LOVE AND CONTROL

LOVE AND CONTROL

The Contemporary Problem

by His Eminence
LÉON JOSEPH CARDINAL SUENENS
Archbishop of Malines-Brussels

THE NEWMAN PRESS
WESTMINSTER · MARYLAND

This translation of *Un problème crucial: Amour et Maîtrise de Soi* (Desclée de Brouwer, Bruges, Paris) was made by GEORGE J. ROBINSON.

NIHIL OBSTAT: CAROLUS DAVIS, S.T.L.
CENSOR DEPUTATUS
IMPRIMATUR: E. MORROGH BERNARD
VICARIUS GENERALIS
WESTMONASTERII: DIE 19a DECEMBRIS 1960

The Nihil obstat *and* Imprimatur *are a declaration that a book or pamphlet is considered to be free from doctrinal or moral error. It is not implied that those who have granted the* Nihil obstat *and* Imprimatur *agree with the contents, opinions or statements expressed.*

First published 1961
Second, revised, edition 1962
Seventh American printing 1965
Eighth American printing 1965

CONTENTS

Chapter   *Page*

Preface   7

PART I : WHAT ARE WE TO THINK?

I   One of Today's Problems   11

II   A Crucial Problem   26

III Clarifying a Basic Misunderstanding   35

IV   The Absolute Need for Sexual Control   51

V   Double Control in Marriage   66

VI   Gradual Control   77

VII Control and Fertility   88

VIII Self-Control and the Regulation of Births   97

PART II : WHAT IS TO BE DONE?

IX   The Role of the Priest   109

X   The Role of the Doctor   127

XI   The Role of University People and
     Scientists   144

XII The Role of Educators   158

XIII The Role of Catholic Organizations   182

     Conclusion   192

Segretaria di Stato di Sua Santita
N.29268

The Vatican, 5 March 1960

Monseigneur,

The Holy Father has received and is graciously pleased
to accept the tribute of your recent work, *Love and Control:
The Contemporary Problem,* and has entrusted to me the
pleasant task of conveying his thanks for the book and for
the filial letter accompanying it.

You have set forth in language that all can understand
the traditional teaching of the Church on these delicate
problems with particular reference to the teaching of recent
Popes and especially to the encyclical *Casti Connubii* of
H.H. Pius XI together with the numerous addresses of
H.H. Pius XII on this subject. The Holy Father sends you
his paternal congratulations and is pleased to express the
hope that your book will enable numerous readers to understand more fully this teaching on a problem that is so important to the Church and to society.

With personal thanks for the copy sent to me, believe me,
Monseigneur, yours devotedly in Our Lord.

(signed) D. Card. Tardini

PREFACE

THIS book is primarily intended for those who are at all involved in sex education. Whether they are directly involved, as are parents or teachers, or indirectly, but certainly as importantly, as are priests, doctors, scientists and leaders of Catholic organizations—this book is meant for them all. We have these people in mind, all of them, because the problem raised in this book cannot be solved without their co-operation and systematic, organized and sustained efforts.

Our book is also, but less explicitly, addressed to all Christians of good will who are trying loyally to create a harmonious fusion of love and self-control in their married life, and who wish to make love in the state of grace, paying attention, at one and the same time, to the demands of their hearts and the duties imposed upon them by their baptism.

It is an important problem we have in mind, and its roots go deep into the heart of the human condition. It is a problem which tests both human integrity and whatever Christian dynamism there is in modern society. Its effects are beyond numbering, and reach every area of life. We have a duty to face up to the problem. Now, more than ever, silence on the subject is out of place; good Christians are anxious to have counsel, understanding and clear, direct answers. Pascal said that proper thinking is the basis of true morality. Before doing anything, therefore, and to help us work more efficiently, we have to discover the basic

7

principles and plan the steps of our solution. Accordingly, the first part of this book is doctrinal: What are we to think? The second part follows logically : What is to be done?

It has not been our plan to discuss all aspects of this complex subject. Instead, we prefer to outline a few basic attitudes of thought and action, and to draw attention to the breadth and pressing importance of a crucial problem.

Part I

WHAT ARE WE TO THINK?

ONE OF TODAY'S PROBLEMS

The Christian in the World

THE modern Christian is harassed by a double outlook on life—his own, and that of his environment. Christianity teaches him moral standards in which good and evil are determined by a universal law. This law, valid always and everywhere, has its ultimate reference in an Absolute Being, the basis of moral obligation, a Being which Christians call God.

On the other side of the coin, however, the world that the Christian lives in today flaunts a relativity in moral standards which uses a rather sliding scale of varying values to determine the most basic concepts of good and evil. The world denies that it is answerable to God and it discards genuine moral culpability, to the point of throwing out the sense of sin, even. According to the world, man is answerable to himself alone. "Now there is neither good nor evil, nor anyone to command me, since I am a man"—this boast that Orestes makes to Jupiter in Sartre's *The Flies* sums up the emancipation of modern man, who will have nothing to do with any objective and universal law, and who proclaims with Merleau-Ponty that "moral conscience dies at its first direct contact with the Absolute".

Here is further evidence of this relativism, as expressed by one of its spokesmen:

Spiritual values fluctuate as much as currency exchange

rates. There are no longer any external truths. Everyone makes his own way, from day to day, trying his best, every day, to catch hold of that day's truth. ... A good statement of the current opinion of our time is in Marxism's idea of truth in evolution, always *becoming* and somehow always new. Truth is not brittle, but flexible and malleable, as though made of rubber, and one must always be wary of it. Today's truth will not be tomorrow's.[1]

"Truth is not brittle, but flexible and malleable"—that is like talking about a shadow's shadow. When a society does not have unchanging standards and consequently gives up its own moral censor, it is headed for complete confusion. How could it possibly pretend to condemn one era's shocking crimes when a change in public opinion or fashion might praise them tomorrow?

The passage we have quoted above holds the glass up to the world we are living in and reveals its dereliction and moral spinelessness.

In such an atmosphere of independence and complete self-sufficiency, human life itself, in all its various modes from beginning to end—from the unborn child to the despairing suicide—is totally subject to man's whim. By what right could moral relativism forbid men to destroy life, by abortion, or to terminate it by suicide as suits each individual best?

In this atmosphere, the "right to sexual emancipation" is a war-cry of the modern way of thinking, and it is nothing more than the most shameful aspect of man's so-called freedom from "religious alienation", as the marxist would say.

Willy-nilly, today's Christian lives in this infectious atmosphere. No matter where he turns, he runs up against this relativist philosophy of life, and he is bound to question

[1] G. Gusdorf, *Traité de l'existence morale* (Paris, n.d.), p. 18.

himself, sometimes uneasily, about the basis of his own moral life. Sometimes he is very easily tempted to get into step with these ideas. Surrounded by these attitudes day and night, a Christian finds it hard to keep his ideas healthy and to sort the true from the false. All around him, the most sacred values are questioned, and the ideas of good and evil have changed completely. The great temptation is to do what everyone else is doing and claim that the Church is old fashioned and that people have to "get in step with the march of time".

It takes great spiritual strength to withstand this tide of opinion.

Great strength is needed all the more since this wave of sexual emancipation has been greeted with the prestige of pseudo-science, of so-called social progress, and of noisy publicity campaigns. A quick look at the progress of neo-Malthusianism will point out how widespread it is and how deeply-rooted. At the same time, it will become plain how very much this problem figures in the modern scene.

The Neo-Malthusian Atmosphere

We have come a long way since Malthus. Everyone knows how he cried havoc at the frightening prospect of over-population and famine. His own solution to this hypo-thetical problem was a birth control which honoured the moral law. His followers, however, outstripped him and, disregarding morality, promoted a system of birth control dictated solely by eugenic and politico-economic needs.

Nowadays, "neo-Malthusianism" goes even further. Like a river rising far off and bearing down alluvium from every shore, the notion of birth control has picked up philosophic débris in its long course since Malthus and has slowly changed into a new system, with a new jargon. Instead of speaking negatively of "controlling births", it is now the fashion to use a positive expression, "Planned Parenthood", or "Family Planning". We hear also the meaningless phrase, "deliberate, conscious and happy motherhood". A very strong organization, the International Planned Parenthood Federation, has been in existence since its foundation in Stockholm in 1953, and has regular meetings in one or other of the world's large cities in addition to conducting active propaganda activities.

Side by side with this evolution of ideas, the sale of contraceptives has made marked progress both in numbers and in the areas of the world reached. In some places, indeed, it is carried on without the least reticence, quite openly and with the support of legal authority. It might be as well to take a quick look at what has been happening.

England

Because of the nationalization of health services in England, Catholic gynecologists have often been placed in difficult situations. If they want to practise medicine as Catholics, while remaining within the public health service framework, they quickly find themselves in a very embarrassing position.

Dr J. Ryan, of London, has more than once spoken out on this score and, recently, *The Catholic Herald* called attention to the dilemma of Catholic doctors who are legally required to take professional part in a practice forbidden by their conscience.

In another area, however, neo-Malthusianism in England was awarded a striking victory at the last Lambeth Conference of the Anglican Church.

The three hundred and ten Anglican bishops who attended the five-week conference beginning in August 1958 declared :

> The Conference believes that the responsibility for deciding upon the number and frequency of children has been laid upon the consciences of parents everywhere;

that the planning, in such ways as are mutually acceptable to husband and wife in Christian conscience, is a
right and important factor in Christian family life and
should be the result of positive choice before God (*The
Lambeth Conference,* London, 1958, part I, p. 57).

Deliberately vague as it is, this resolution obviously
avoids any objective moral evaluation of the use of contraceptives. But when it mentions acceptable methods, it
implicitly supposes that some couples will choose contraceptives—and it makes no condemnation. It opens the door
to contraception by this omission.

Except in Catholic circles, this attitude seems perfectly
natural, because neo-Malthusian propaganda has had such
a long history in the Anglo-Saxon world. The situation is
the same in other Protestant countries, especially in Scan-
dinavia, where birth control has become as much a part of
life as the laws of hygiene and physical comfort.

The connection between Protestantism and neo-Malthusianism is logically based on the doctrines of Luther and
Calvin. For them, any reference to nature and the natural
law, as a norm of reality, is meaningless, since they consider
that nature has been radically vitiated by Original Sin. It is
a short step, and an easy one, from this attitude to opt for
the "law of Christian liberty" against the natural law,
written in the heart of the human person.

France

Not even countries traditionally Catholic are immune,
however.

In France, March 1955 saw the launching of a Family
Planning Campaign, amid great clamour, by a medical
notice issued by the Academie des Sciences Politiques et
Morales. The French press devoted a lot of space and comment to the notice. Support and propaganda for the campaign were further brought to bear by Jacques Derogy's

book, *Des enfants malgré nous*. Even parliamentary circles felt the effects of the movement: a suggested bill was brought to the office of the National Assembly, and its purpose, according to the introductory remarks, was "to forestall the growth of criminal abortion by means of anti-conceptive prophylaxis". The remedy it suggested was the abrogation of articles 3 and 4 in the French law of 31 July 1920, articles which suppressed neo-Malthusian propagandizing.

The suggestion has not got any further but, despite the incontestable rise in the French birth-rate, contraception has made a telling incursion into the country's way of life.

The instability of family life and the disturbing increase of divorces can, of course, be traced back to the corrosive and shattering effect of contraception. One out of every ten French marriages ends in divorce, and more than one out of every five such cases occur in the Department of the Seine.

These figures give a good idea of the instability which sin brings into the home. A free-thinking attitude towards God's law about child-bearing quickly and easily leads to an emancipated point of view towards the permanence of marriage and the eventual rupture of the marriage bond. Sin breeds sin, surely and predictably. When the home falls from the state of God's grace, it runs the risk of collapse before the eyes of men as well.

Belgium

Belgium, too, is running the same course as France. Any enquiry into the reasons for de-Christianization, or loss of faith, particularly in urban communities, will soon bring up the question whether many people, baptized as infants, do not fall away from the Church because of birth control. No one, of course, fails to realize that there are some couples who are childless despite their own wishes.

Nevertheless, the statistics available, which are concerned with the overall situation rather than individual instances, paint a depressing picture : families with three or more children do not make up even a fourth of all Belgian families, whereas the infant mortality rate is 16.64 per thousand, one of the lowest in the world. The significance of these figures is enhanced when we reflect that, in Belgium, divorce—a good barometer of the religious atmosphere and family life in a country—grows daily. Some figures give one divorce out of every four marriages in some urban centres, and seven out of every hundred for the entire country. Surely this is convincing proof that the evil is widespread and dangerous, and the causes deep-rooted.

Although the other Catholic European countries, Italy, Spain, Portugal, Ireland, have so far withstood the neo-Malthusian onslaught, for various reasons which we cannot touch on here, their resistance is only relative and the struggle to achieve sound family life is far from being won.

The United States of America

The neo-Malthusian spirit has infected America and Asia as well as Europe.

In the United States, the movement has taken every opportunity to influence legislation pertaining to public health organizations.

Resistance is strong among American Catholics, but is hardly met with in many Protestant circles.

A recent, typical example was the birth control controversy in New York City's hospitals. The outcome of this affair was a memorandum, issued by the Bureau of Hospitals of the City of New York, setting out the conditions under which birth control might be permitted. The memorandum was publicly rejected and repudiated by a declaration issued jointly by the Archdiocese of New York and the Diocese of Brooklyn.

The question even assumed political importance.

The American Senator William Fulbright, chairman of the Senate Foreign Affairs Committee, recently made public a report recommending a system of mechanical contraception which could be put into use in countries where no religious restrictions against such practices exist. Prepared for Senator Fulbright by the Standard Research Institute, the report outlines the method for bringing this campaign into conjunction with United States world politics.

Further, all American Catholic newspapers recently reported and commented upon the protests made to the President's consultative commission which was formed to revise the objectives of America's foreign military and economic aid, and which was strongly considering a programme to promote birth control.

Japan

In Asia, Japan and India are the two countries farthest advanced in the matter of systematized birth control.

On 28 June 1948, the Japanese Diet passed a "Law for Eugenic Protection", under whose protection birth control gained a strong foothold. The law authorized the sale of contraceptives and the government itself undertook to instruct the Japanese people in birth control methods. There are about seven consulting centres where these methods are taught.

A consulting specialist in Tokyo recently sent me his observations:

> Birth control has become fairly widespread. From its ratio of fifteen per cent in 1950, and almost thirty per cent in 1953, it has increased to fifty or sixty per cent at the present. And one can give this figure without fear of exaggeration.

Information clinics have increased in the poorest areas, and they afford free consultation as well as provide contraceptive devices free of charge. Specially trained social workers visit homes—sometimes uninvited—to instruct wives. Factory directors and managers have started to apply more and more pressure to get their workers to limit the size of their families.

The result of this campaign is a gradual lowering of the birth rate which, in 1957, fell to 17.2 per thousand inhabitants, whereas, before the introduction of birth control, it was thirty per thousand. This new, low rate is not the result of contraceptive practices alone, but of legal and illegal abortions as well which, according to official estimates, have reached one million.

India

During the Congress of the All India Conference of Family Planning, in January 1957, Colonel Barkat Narain, a special government consultor, announced that the government was going to set up two thousand rural centres for instruction in family planning methods. Fifty thousand villages and five hundred and sixty urban areas were visited by government propaganda teams during that same year. The plan was to establish a birth control centre for every thousand people within five years. One cannot help thinking that the Indian people's traditional morality, so energetically expounded and taught by Gandhi and his followers, was systematically being broken down and was daily losing ground.

Dr Chandrasekhar, director of the Indian Institute for Population Studies, a member of Unesco, stated at the University of Hong Kong that the Indian authorities envisaged giving the equivalent of seventeen dollars to every man with two children and with a monthly income less than three hundred and twelve dollars, who would agree to be sterilized.

In his book on India's population, Dr Chandrasekhar made the following significant comment:

> The population question is the crux of India's national economic problem. At this rate, according to some calculations, India may reach the staggering figure of some 600,000,000 by A.D. 2001 .... The only remedy everyone talks about is that of growing more food as though India's land and sea frontiers could be extended or the yield per acre could be doubled overnight. If India is unable to feed her people at the present miserable level of nutrition with imports, how is she going to feed them without imports and that at a higher level of consumption, if the population continues to increase at about 4,000,000 a year? ... If the country does succeed in growing more food, about five million tons within the next year, the present imports can be dispensed with. But this will not solve the problem of increasing the per capita consumption, much less raising the general standard of living, for there will be another four million extra mouths to feed. The problem will become all the more intractable when our public health services are improved, bringing down the present uncivilised mortality rate. As our public health and environmental hygiene improve, the death rate is bound to come down sparing more mouths to feed.
>
> The Government must distribute contraceptive literature with the ration card. ...[1]

We shall not discuss the demographic aspects of the problem here. Father Stanislas de Lestapis, S. J., has already done it with rare ability and a complete sensitivity to the problem in his recent book.[2]

[1] S. Chandrasekhar, *India's Population: Fact and Policy*, Indian Institute for Population Studies, Annamalai University, Chidambaran, India, 1950, pp. 17, 22, 122-3.
[2] *Family Planning and Modern Problems: A Catholic Analysis*, London, Burns & Oates, 1961.

With statistical figures at his fingertips, he analyzes every argument proffered and suggests other, morally acceptable, means of controlling a too-high birth rate. This, for example, is one of his suggestions:

> It has been shown that to raise *the age at which women marry*—and in Asia they marry very young—would, if it could be done, of itself bring about a substantial decrease in fertility. It is well known, as a result of the detailed enquiries of J. N. Sinha at Bangalore (1951), that in this town marriages of over fifteen years duration produced an average of 6.4 children per family when the mother had married before the age of 14, 6 children when she had married between 14 and 16, 5.3 children when she had married between 18 and 21, and 3.5 children when she had married after the age of 21. In a word, if the marriage age of young women is raised by 8 years India might succeed in reducing her fertility rate by 30 per cent.[1]

We cite this observation of Father de Lestapis simply as a warning sign against the naïveté of neo-Malthusian claims. A comparison between the average ages at which Indian girls—a little more than fourteen—and European and Western girls—about 21.7 in England, 22.6 in France, 23.9 in Austria and 24.35 in Norway—marry, shows very clearly how important this point is.

But the fact needs stressing that this is only one facet of a very complex problem which can only be solved by working through the many aspects of international aid to under-developed countries.

There is an Irish proverb that says, "When God shuts a door, He always opens a window." Since some avenues out of this problem are closed by morality, it is up to men to look for other, acceptable, solutions, keeping it always in

[1] S. de Lestapis, S.J., *op. cit.*, pp. 246-7.

mind that, in the last resort, respect for the natural law is the surest way to protect and ensure the true life of a nation.

* * *

The Neo-Malthusian Platform

This quick sketch has given some idea of how widespread neo-Malthusianism is and to what extent it poses a problem to the modern Christian. Being surrounded by an enemy makes it more difficult to fight him. But the fight is harder when the enemy makes good use of the terrain. Thus, for instance, neo-Malthusianism takes advantage of man's deep thirst for a sexual life free of any moral restraint, and of the fact that this instinct becomes the more ruthless and disorderly the more it is yielded to.

There are other, more extrinsic, factors which bolster the campaign of this destructive attitude.

Standard of Living and Comfort

One thing that neo-Malthusianism has in its favour is the modern excessive anxiety to raise the standard of living and to achieve greater comfort. More and more, parents want more than simply to bring children into the world. They want to assure their education and their future, and quite rightly, too. They also want their children to enjoy a higher social position than they themselves do. All this is quite normal, but there is a strong temptation to limit the number of children, regardless of the means, so that this goal can be achieved, no matter what.

It would be as well to recall here that the Church has never divorced the ideas of procreation and education. Bringing up children, in the basic meaning of the phrase, has always been part of what the Church considers the procreative process and human education. But, here as everywhere else, the end does not justify the means.

There is, however, more to the situation than simply this eagerness for betterment at any cost. An exaggerated attachment to comfort plays a subtle and undermining role. The modern world is off on a frenzied search for material pleasure, to exactly the extent, indeed, as it lacks the largeness of spirit it needs to control technical progress. Because of this delight in comfort, the inconveniences brought on by the birth of a child seem greater than they used to. Not the least of these is a curtailment of the parents' freedom to do those things which are becoming more and more popular: travel, parties, residence abroad, etc. The consideration of comfort has even, in some cases, taken the first place in some people's plans. Everyone has heard of couples torn between the choice of a car or a child, or a holiday at the sea or another child.

The Housing Problem

Though it is true that too much emphasis on the "good things of life" can damage moral standards, still there is a minimum of comfort and the rest which is essential. This is especially true in regard to the housing problem which is almost desperate in some countries and larger cities.

In Paris, thirty-five per cent of the city's one million, one hundred and sixty-seven thousand families live in one room, twenty-six per cent have two rooms. Behind these bare figures there are details and stories which would fill many, many books.

Besides, think of all the people who live in makeshift huts, in work camps where the conditions are far below human, or—far worse—in the streets.

One has only to look at the great buildings of the world's largest cities to see that they are like mammoth advertising hoardings, with neo-Malthusian theses inscribed deep in the steel and concrete.

Still, comparing the two evils, exaggerated riches and

comfort, and devastating poverty, we must concede that the zeal for wealth is a more fertile ground for neo-Malthusianism than is the shame of being poor.

Woman's New Position and a More Personal Approach to Marriage

So far, we have discussed this problem from its economic angle; now let us take a look at the social and psychological factors involved.

One of the most striking developments of our era has been the gradually increasing emancipation of women. In Christian countries, it is now unheard of that women should be subjected to the many kinds of slavery and subjection in which many of them still live in pagan areas.

This development is good, if only because it has opened up to women many areas of social activity where they have worked wonders. On the other hand, there has been the concomitant danger that many women have lost their own realization of their role as mothers. One bad sort of feminism has drawn women's attention to those people who promote regulated motherhood, or so-called happy motherhood. The idea of a woman as a mother is losing ground; at its worst, legitimate ambition sometimes ends with a woman's denial of her true being and a rejection of the role which only she can, and should, play in the human context.

Another consideration is the advance made by the idea, good in itself, of personal love in marriage. Marriage used to be a strictly social institution which, for that reason, was more often of greater interest to parents than to young people. Today, we no longer accept the idea of marriages "arranged" to meet parents' social and economic ambitions and needs.

The idea of love has become all-important. This, too, is a good thing, but it may involve the temptation to adjust the married state to the couple's own, personal goals, thereby minimizing its social purpose, procreation.

All these factors, innocent enough in themselves and each a feature of the progressive humanization of marriage, nevertheless conspire to build up an atmosphere in which neo-Malthusian ideas are either adopted wholeheartedly or are granted a more tolerant hearing than they deserve. Besides all this, the Christian notion of marriage is besieged from all sides by the modern means of communication—newspapers, films, radio—which endlessly stimulate an obsessive interest in the erotic, to the disadvantage of love's real meaning and nature. By now it must be clear why we have to come to grips with this problem.

Chapter II

A CRUCIAL PROBLEM

SEXUAL emancipation and the way that it has shown itself, particularly in deliberate, and wrong, contra-ceptive practices, is a crucial problem involving man's social, family and religious life and behaviour as well as his private activity. At this point it may be well to spend some time thinking about this effect in the religious sphere, especially.

Sexual Morality and Alienation from Religion

We do not need figures or graphs to show us how serious the problem is. It would be enough to go into a church some Sunday and count the number of people there and the age groups they represent.

Where, in many traditionally Catholic countries, are the adults, especially men between the ages of twenty-five and fifty, who are faithful to their religious duties? What pro-portion are they of regular church-goers? How many of them go to Holy Communion?

Granting that the numbers will vary according to the religious spirit of different regions, one thing is always the same—the disproportion is large and shocking.

Why is there this defection, this saddening desertion? Is there any reason, a subtle and hidden reason perhaps, why so many people are alienated from the Sacraments, if not from the Church? Is it rash to suggest that, in many instances, Christian morality's restrictive control of people's sexual activity is the stumbling block?

Accepting this restrictive control comes down to admitting that the natural instinct for enjoying unlimited sexual pleasure must be harnessed and put in its proper place in human life by making it subordinate to the orders of an intellect illumined by grace. In other words, it means realizing that the body should submit to the soul, and the soul to God. It means recognizing humbly God's law working within and upon our own living, dynamic bodies. Of course, we cannot achieve this attitude without a struggle which can sometimes threaten Christian living and rock it to its foundations. When we do stop using thought to guide our life, we begin guiding our thoughts by the way we live.

Without implying that it is the one and only reason why so many give up religion, we must admit that the rejection of the Church's teaching on sex has a great deal to do with this process of religious defection. For the fact is that people are not only giving up frequenting the Sacraments, they are forgetting about personal and family religious life as well. Once a man reaches this crossroads and breaks with the Church, though he may once have been faithful to his duties, he gradually gives up all prayer-life and living contact with God. Like a plant cut off from sunlight, his prayer-life dwindles once it loses touch with the dynamic force of community prayer in the sacrifice of the altar. A man and woman stop turning their interior gaze towards God in heaven, and their life becomes earth-bound, losing everything but its earthly, horizontal dimension. Very often, they not only forget about the Church, but even go for days without even thinking of God. Where does family prayer fit into this sort of life, and how can children receive a Christian education in this environment?

As the separation from God and His grace grows, there is also, obvious and conscious or not, a gradual alienation of the couple from one another. For God only is the foundation of their love and the seal of their union. Sin which penetrates to the most intimate areas of married love is corrosive and slowly eats away at marital fidelity itself. Left on their own, human affections are too easily prey to fickleness. Love which is to be strong and constant needs every bit of divine charity it can get, the heart must learn to love even as God loves.

In view of all this no one, surely, is taken by surprise by the incredible spread of divorce, the modern world's plague.

In Sweden, for example, divorce is becoming disconcertingly frequent. One hundred years ago, the divorce rate was four per cent of the number of marriages; in 1900, it had risen to fourteen per cent, and now there are fifty divorces for every hundred marriages. A closer look at statistics shows that in Stockholm, for instance, forty-eight per cent of the couples married longer than four years are either divorced or seeking divorces.

These figures and similar figures that could be adduced for U.S.A. and (to a lesser extent) for England and a number of other Western countries, show quite clearly where religious indifference leads. Once loyalty to God has been thrown over and we feel free of His law, how can any vows, no matter how sacred they are, expect loyalty in the face of temptation and passion?

Does anyone understand completely the havoc wrought by divorce? If, as almost always happens, the divorce is followed by remarriage, the immobility of spiritual death sets in. Living in an unreal situation falsifies judgments and attitudes. Social life is overwhelmed by an avalanche of sins, inevitably growing in number and seriousness. When a family is broken up, it is not simply a question of two people who no longer live together, but a home is destroyed and children set adrift. People are constantly expressing anxiety over the growth of juvenile delinquency; but investigations show that the root of juvenile crime is in a lack of love in the home or, even worse, in the lack of a real home. These young people who are rebels against society are, first of all, the victims of a revolt against God which passion has instigated. Even without going that far, however, we can nevertheless say that a child who is denied the chance to grow up in an atmosphere of life and unity is handicapped for life, like a bud blighted by frost.

Sin is like a stone thrown into a pool: its effect spreads in ever-widening concentric circles. Every sin committed, even in secret, leaves its mark on society. Satan increases his grip on the world with every sin. The only way to kill the social evil that is divorce and to scotch the spread of its infection is to get at its root. We cannot help recognizing how evil a thing sexual emancipation is—its effects are too evil for that. It has brought up problems which must be dealt with in the interests of man's religious welfare, as well as simply for his general good.

When people leave the Church because "she doesn't understand love", they too often give this reason as justification for an attitude which denies the Church any competence in this field, which, they insist, is a matter of individual conscience.

Restricting the Church this way, of course, comes down to denying basic Christianity. No one denies that a man's first obligation is to his conscience. But that is just the point: if a man follows his conscience and remains in the Church, then he should also follow his conscience and accept the Church's teaching. There is no place for conscientious objectors in the Church who accept only part or reject part of what she teaches. Heresy means a withdrawal. Taking or leaving doctrines as one chooses is a basic denial of the essential meaning of the Church and her divine foundation. As Father Congar has said, the faithful must be free within the Church, but not with regard to the Church.

All this, of course, does not at all mean that personal conscience plays no part in making real the demands and limitations laid on it by Christian morality. But this must be done within the Church and her context, not in any fringe-areas. As a soul grows in purity and refinement, its conscience suggests more and more sensitive and delicate ways to practise virtue. But these ways must be compatible with fundamental principles. There are many ways of interpreting a sonata; each of them, nevertheless, must respect the original score.

People's refusal to abide by the Church's sex teachings is something like what happened when our Lord announced the institution of the Eucharist to the people who were with Him in the desert. "This is a hard saying," they said, "and who can stand it?" But then Christ tested His apostles' confidence in Him and asked, "Will you also go away?" Peter's answer was a proclamation of fidelity: "Lord, to whom shall we go? You have the words of eternal life." The Christian, though he may not understand everything, cannot make any other, valid answer.

Thus it is, then, a crossroads, a decisive choice—and the future of religious life in the family depends on how the choice is made.

* * *

Sexual Morality and Integral Christianity

Important as it is for people who leave the Church, the choice is just as important, though in a different way, for those who remain faithful, for those homes truly Christian and for apostolic families especially.

We should thank heaven that there are a lot of apostolic families. It is largely to the credit of our young people's Catholic Action groups and the Young Christian Workers movement that they exist. They are the present joy of the Church and her hope for the future, and her bond with them has grown up out of confidence and candour. But this bond is also a dialogue based on these families' desire for instruction: they want honest and frank instruction; they want to integrate their spiritual life with married life; they want to be truly Christian, not only on Sundays and in Church, but always, everywhere and especially in their home life and their married life; they want to bring the logical conclusions of their baptism into their daily life; finally, they realize that Christ is not merely the life of the soul but the life of the whole man, and that every bit of the Gospels must be put into every bit of life.

Far from accusing the Church of intruding into their private life, these families insist that she exercise a maternal care and interest in their affairs. They want the Church to examine closely their most intimate problems, to understand those frequently painful situations which they become involved in, and to give them firm and rapid solutions to problems troubling their conscience. They want the Church to point out a single, straight and direct route through life's too often complicated reality.

These families want to be listened to, they want to be able to explain their difficulties, to put moralists' theories side by side with their own experience of life, and to co-operate in the specific and pertinent application of those parts of the Church's doctrine which affect them more than anyone else.

They rightly feel that it is in this area, especially, that the co-operation of the laity is most valuable. They consider it part of their pledge to live full Christian lives in the world.

This is a crucial problem because it affects the atmosphere within a Christian home, but also because it conditions the apostolic effectiveness of these families. They are not interested in living completely Christian lives for their own sakes alone; they want to share this integralness with other people. They feel that a community of interest in family living is as important as common interests in other apostolic activities. The apostolate of the home has achieved the

importance and dignity of other apostolic work, which is as
varied as human life and experience. To a great extent,
sound family life is an operative factor in re-Christianizing
the world, since it is a concrete manifestation of lives built
upon and dependent on true Christian love.

*   *   *

The Church's Involvement

The Church is, in her own way, as deeply involved in
this question as are individual Christians. It is, after all,
a matter of how successful her apostolates will be, and how
and to what extent her growth will be influenced. Because
of our Lord's mandate, "Go, and teach the gospel to all
creatures," the Church must bring all men to God and
make Christ welcome in every home. She must go along
the "highways and by-ways" to bring men to sharing God's
life. But they cannot live this way unless they are living in
the state of grace.

This last is the crucial point. Every priest has had experience of a certain type of Easter confession : if such confessions are honest, it is clear that some change must be
made in the penitent's married life; if they are not honest
—the penitent fools no one but himself. Obviously the
Church finds herself in a difficult position. How can she
end her maternal invitation to forgiveness and reconciliation
by refusing absolution? At all costs, she must take the lead
in apostolic activity and sex education, otherwise all her
work will come to nothing.

Her apostolic growth is involved; but, even more, her
growth in numbers itself is at stake, because every attempt
to frustrate the real end of married love reduces the
Church's potential size. How can we hope for vocations to
the priesthood and the religious life, vocations which are
so sorely needed, if families, which should be the seed beds

of vocations, are consumed by a blind opposition to God's law? Vocations must be tended as one cares for rare and valuable plants.

A glance at statistics makes it clear that vocations come from families where home life is realistic and healthy. Anything that harms this atmosphere strikes at the heart of vocation. Contrariwise, whatever helps a family to remain in the state of grace also leaves it open to the wonderful possibility of a vocation to the priesthood. Matrimony and Holy Orders are Sacraments which complement one another perfectly. A marriage can have no better outcome than to have one of its sons become a priest, and that priest will be the pride and glory of his family. St Pius X's mother once said to him, "You wouldn't be wearing that ring if I hadn't had my ring first."

Our present Holy Father wanted to underline this relationship when, asked what name he would take as pope, he said John, because it had been his father's name. By this touching gesture of love for his father, he highlighted the relation between the two Sacraments. Over and above all this, the notion of priestly celibacy is a manifestation of the link between the two Sacraments because when a man becomes a priest and consequently gives up his right to marry, he does it as an act of human love so that, freely and lovingly, he may act as a spiritual father to all those families placed in his care. From this angle as well, then, a healthy religious atmosphere in the home is essential if we want a continually-growing Christianity.

But if the situation is so bad in Christian countries, and is such a threat to the life and growth of the Church, it assumes almost incredible proportions in mission areas. Imagine the job faced by missioners in underdeveloped countries like India where the whole country is in the grip of organized family planning! Because these countries often suffer from famine and because their standard of living seems to drop as their birth rate climbs, the missioners' problem seems to be thinking and rethinking the whole business of conversion and evangelization.

There is no need to spend more time on this point, but it is worth while thinking about the religious aspects of the problem and to what extent it is a *crucial problem*.

On the Way to a Solution

From what we have said it must be clear that the Church cannot disassociate herself from this problem; it is a question of the future of family life and, therefore, of her own future. *Pro aris et focis*—for the altar and for the home; the two ideas are tightly linked.

But conjugal morality is only one aspect of the larger problem of man's control of himself in the area of sexuality. We cannot expect a solution to a problem which has not been raised. Nor can we give offhand solutions to problems whose solution needs instruction and education. Trite and neat little answers will not do when we are called upon to point out a way to harmonize the demands of truth and the principles of love and life. No one can give a quick answer to any of life's problems; the wise man will try to be ready with an answer before the problem arises. Sexual education is one of these problems whose answers need long, previous reflection.

Men have to be taught control over their sexual instincts. This is the only really humane and Christian answer to the problem of love.

But before going into the "how" and "why" of this control, perhaps we should examine more closely the meaning of a word we have been using very much so far—love.

Chapter III

CLARIFYING A BASIC
MISUNDERSTANDING

SOMEONE once asked a wise man of China what he would do if he were made ruler of the world. "I should bring words back to their original meanings," he replied. And what a boon to the world that would be!

It is a fact, it always has been and it still is, that some words have a personal history of their own and, as time goes on, are influenced by current philosophies, picking up new or modified meanings much as batteries pick up and store electricity. *Love* is one of those words. Its meaning today has been influenced by the modern world's highly charged erotic atmosphere. To accept its meaning on those grounds is to miss getting the whole picture.

As Catholics, our greatest difficulty, perhaps, is to be the leaven in our modern world without being contaminated by that world. The same thing applies to the words we use. Every once in a while we should take stock of our vocabulary and see if it needs sharpening-up—or pruning.

We talk about "orthodoxy", the "reunion of the Churches" and "civil marriage", among other things, and we have adopted modern meanings for those words. We must be constantly on the look-out to keep our use of such words sharp and free from any modern ambiguity. So-called "orthodoxy" is not orthodoxy; the "reunion of the Churches" is meaningless unless it refers to a return to unity within the One, True Church; "civil marriage", so far as a baptized person is concerned, is valid only as the civil formalization of a religious ceremony and has no other validity. We have to go through this sharpening-up of words and their meanings especially when we come to the word "love" which by this time has all sorts of connotations of affectivity and nobility. This is a job which we expect our teachers, our Catholic Action leaders and our authors to take on. One newspaper-writer recently told me, "Today we call 'crimes of love' what used to be called 'tragedies of misconduct'." It is easy to see the shift of public opinion and notice where it warps. A very old maxim says : *Principiis obsta*—Resistance should start at the beginning. We can ring the changes on that and say that our battle begins at the very beginning with words and their meanings.

Some of the Church's critics insist that she is the enemy of love. They are right, if they mean what they call love. Christians, however, have to be careful not to be fooled and to grasp these people's real meaning; do they mean the same thing as we do when they talk about the "demands of love"? Or is there a basic and initial vagueness, a shift of emphasis, between the two meanings? We are not simply quibbling over words, but underlining a basic misunderstanding which has to be cleared up before our battle can begin. Giving in about the meaning of a word can often mean compromising one's position. No one wants to fight under his enemy's colours; the word "love" has a human and Christian meaning which on no account must be muddled. The word has deviated from its original meaning so that, today, it is the wrapping about shoddy and inferior goods.

A Profound Meaning

"Words are like battles," a famous general once said, "the right word is a battle won, an inaccurate word is a defeat."

For today's Christian, the word "love" is a defeat whose

losses must be recouped. The fact is that no other word has been so weakened and muddled by modern literature and the jargon used by television, radio, films and advertising. Newspapers and magazines are filled with it; every page has "all the facts" about its "amazing powers" and the crimes it inspires. Every day and all day, the radio broadcasts it, with or without music, on every wave length. The cinemas give us love scenes lasting almost as long as entire films. Many plays revolve about it as their theme, and the advertising world has undertaken to bring its "new image" to the world.

"Love" is put forth as the one excuse which makes any sort of behaviour blameless, and which is its own justification. When a man is overwhelmed by desire for someone else's wife, he justifies his liberty by appealing to "love". People use it to cover up the most disgraceful conduct. But that is not real love; it is nothing more than blinding physical passion. "Love" is used as an alibi, a cover-up for the most cynical selfishness, misconduct, adultery, impurity. It would be a good thing if Catholic publicists put the word between inverted commas every time "love" was used as a blind for a reality which is the negation of love. As much as possible, they should "call a spade a spade" and thus, by a sort of reverse incantation, strip away the magical power the word now has to disguise a reality far more brutal than it appears.

"Ah, Love, what crimes have been committed in thy name!" It is now the fashion to pretend that adultery and fornication are effects of an uncontrollable instinct, a power which is irresistible. This kind of "love", in fact, is only cowardice and disloyalty, a breaking of vows and a refusal to act justly towards the people to whom we owe justice. The word's dignity should not hide the ugliness of the actions it stands for. No one calls a smirk a smile, so why call "love" what is its very counterfeit?

Sometimes, however, "love" does not mean what is really its opposite, but the modern world confuses part for whole and applies the term to what is really only an aspect of love, or one of its composite emotions.

Frequently, people talk about love and mean sexual pleasure. There is this constant confusion between the two and it is so widespread that even Christians sometimes fail to distinguish the two properly. This confused carelessness about essentials is the central point about which the modern world's secularization of love revolves. But we shall return to this point later. Love seems to have become so worldly that we often feel embarrassed when discussing the Church's teaching on the subject with a certain type of Christian. They think that the Church has nothing to do with it, and that the spontaneity of love makes it its own legislator, immune from external influence.

What people have done, of course, is to limit love to its lowest level of meaning and effectiveness, and then deliberately to keep it there. But it is up to us, on the other hand, to restore everything to its proper place, emphasizing the true hierarchy of values and putting things back into relation with their sources and causes. Charles Moeller put it very well when, discussing the subject of love, he wrote, "The evil of impurity consists in its being one of the chief repudiations of genuine love."

It is in trickery like this we have been discussing that we recognize the work of him whom Scripture calls the Father of Lies. We must cast out this deception by which the Children of Darkness make fools of the Children of Light. Our job is to restore to real love its pristine and sacred meaning.

Love's Divine Dimensions
Love is the purest reflection of God. Indeed, it is God living in men's hearts.

St John tells us that "God is love". It is the basis of the Divine Existence, its definition and its expression. All being flows from Love as from its wellspring, and everything has Love as ultimate end and goal. As He created us "outside" Himself, God, at the same instant, put that in us which would make us always turn back to Him. Children play with boomerangs, throwing them so that they return to them, and this is an analogy of man's life in respect to God.

God made us to His image and likeness, and made our hearts like His own. Human experience is the best and surest proof of this truth of faith, and shows just how avidly man turns to Love.

Ask any man what his deepest desire is. What does he want on earth, what is he looking for? On the surface, men's desires and ambitions are many and seem to be different from one another: business, politics, art, literature, working on the land, sailing the high seas, or flying through the skies.

But actually, beneath appearances and apparent differences, what all men are looking for is something simple in itself and very touching: they want to love and to be loved. All men hunger and thirst after true love, love which knows no time, suffers no wear, lasts endlessly. They are looking for a motive of life proportioned to the capacity of their hearts. Music and songs are filled with mankind's nostalgia for infinite and eternal love. Men sometimes fall into disgrace in their search for love, but they go on looking unstintingly.

Without realizing it, men are looking for Love in their search to love and be loved; they are seeking that single, Infinite and Eternal Love, which is God and which they seek in human creatures. But is it strange that a stream should remember its source? Was not man born of Love, God, before he was born of his father and mother? Does not God's creative paternity come first in the phenomena of human generation?

God's paternity is richer than we at first imagine, because it is the source of a Trinitarian love. We think about this and the dimensions of Divine Love expand until they go beyond our understanding.

God is not a lonely God; this truth of revelation implies a world of joy. It would be difficult to understand a God who was a single person. Faith reveals the Trinity to us and plunges us into a great world of illuminating mystery, paradoxical as it may be. God is a society of Persons. He is known infinitely, as it is fitting that He be known, in His Son. He is also infinitely loved, in proportion to His infinite Goodness, in the Holy Spirit. In God, there is a threefold, mutual impetus, from the Father towards the Son, from the Son towards the Father, and from the Father and the Son to Their common Spirit. This triple impulse, personal and subsistent, unites the Three Persons in the purest form of self-giving, the most sharply defined *ecstasy* of auto-donation. Nothing hinders this activity; one poet has said that the Trinity and Its mutual dynamic relationships are each like "a bird who would be pure flight". God is complete living communion, perfect reciprocal exchange. He is a simultaneous giving and taking of love—the Father and the Son—and He is reciprocal Love, lived and experienced in that reciprocity itself. He is Spirit.

Sometimes simple people understand things better than the learned : a good, simple Christian once said, "Love is such a big thing in our lives that I understand how in God it may be Somebody". It is this kind of reflection that helps us realize that the human heart was created in the image of the Trinity Itself; it bears the mark of the life of the Trinity, and therein has its highest distinction.

From all this, then, it is not surprising that the Church takes her place in the world as the incorruptible guardian of love, and that she keeps a jealous eye on love's sacred character. She has assumed nothing but what is her rightful position. Christians, more than anyone else, must always remind themselves that the Church has found the secret of real love in the very heart of God.

But how the Church has to struggle to continue as rightful trustee of this heritage! All around her there are hundreds of publications which devote their time to debasing love, approve of and encourage divorce and would like to soil the purity of love with their filth and trash. Like the Jews, who were chosen by God to preserve monotheism in a world filled with idolatry, the Church stands out as the only guardian of real integral and indissoluble love. In a world which mixes its denial of love with blasphemy of God, the Church goes on, like the ancient Ark, weathering the stormy and violent waves. We speak of "the prophetic mission of Christian families to the world"; these families must be witnesses to Love working amongst men, they have to teach men how to love.

Love's Human Dimensions

We have to understand love's divine aspect, as proceeding from God, but we must also consider all its human aspects and dimensions, because there is even a tendency to minimize its scope and breadth on this level, too. Love is very complex, and when we discuss it our words must be able to give an idea of this complexity. Educators can never stress too much the balancing power that love has, nor the harmony it creates which unites all sorts of differences and without which love would be something else, crippled, mutilated, betrayed.

True love between husband and wife implies a communion of souls, in which they are one in mind, heart and body. When we speak of a communion of souls we mean that they each make their deepest inner life common and shared, exchanging their most secret and intimate thoughts. A communion of minds means that they both think the same way about the basic problems of life, sharing a common viewpoint on living and the whole business of life. Communion of hearts means reciprocal affection, each giving self to the other, "paying undivided attention to the other's existence". The communion of bodies is physical union, a translation into physical terms of the sharing of the soul's life and of the blending affections.

The modern world has not enough esteem for this very necessary harmony. It underestimates the first two aspects, and overestimates the latter two. The accent is all on physical union when moderns talk about "love", even if the other three features are missing. This is an abuse of language, a word game.

There is, however, an even more serious aspect to it than this deliberate oversight of some of the basic aspects of love's communion. Too often, when people discuss love and mean only physical union, what they really mean is simply genital union. The result is that, in the long run, "love" means physical pleasure, a direct or indirect stimulation of orgasm. Here we have reached the lowest level of love's profanation.

It might be well to notice here that "sexual" and "genital" do not mean the same thing. Men and women, masculine and feminine, are distinguished by their physical and moral sexual differences. In this sense, sexuality belongs to the body as a whole and in all its parts—a single drop of blood can be analyzed to determine if it is from a man or a woman. On the other hand, the word "genital" refers to one area only of the entirety, it denotes those parts only of the body which are designed for sexual reproduction.

When we said that many people speak of physical communion and really mean genital union, we certainly did not mean to imply that this is their deliberate and conscious motivation during a long process which is accompanied by affection and emotion. The desire for this pleasure can be so strong, however, that it is allowed to exclude any other deliberate or indeliberate motivations. Modern man too often exalts the need to love in this way and insists that this need is so powerful that it is something which has a concomitant absolute right to expression, a right which must not be "interfered" with by the Church. This sort of "love", he insists, is perfectly and essentially expressed in genital pleasure.

Now this confusion is very serious. Anyone who has anything at all to do with teaching others what real love is should know about it and be on guard against it. We must clear up this basic ambiguity and distinguish very clearly between love and genital pleasure which, in clearly determined circumstances, may but need not be love's legitimate accompaniment.

The Catholic position should be made clear on all these points and distinctions. Every attempt to do so has not been successful. One Catholic weekly, for instance, gave this unfortunate résumé of what is called the Church's teaching : "While the Church's adversaries propose the complete satisfaction of man's instincts, the Church herself insists that instinct must be governed by the will, by conscience and the intellect. *She does not admit that love can be divorced from procreation.* It is futile to expect that she will eventually change her attitude on this point. She cannot, any more than she can allow divorce or abortion."

The sentence in italics is wrong and unfortunate. The writer meant that no separation can be made between the genital pleasure we have been discussing and procreation. Fundamentally, he was right, but he erred when he used the word "love" to mean such pleasure. Basically, love is one thing, procreation another.

It is of the utmost importance that Christian teachers

and writers strike out against the misunderstanding and confusion which deceive and ensnare consciences. It is up to them to help people understand that this sort of pleasure is not, contrary to what so many believe, the highest expression of love, nor its only manifestation, nor, indeed, its essential and necessary manifestation.

When we put human love into a context where it means only the physical gestures and act of married love, we betray a basic misunderstanding of what love really is. Reacting against Manichaeism's and Jansenism's contempt for the body, some works of modern literature have tried to put forth physical union as the highpoint of married life and the last word on love. By doing this, however, they oversimplify the essential complexity of married love and, by approaching the matter from this angle, they get a distorted picture of the complete reality.

At this point, therefore, it might be a good idea to take a look at some of the contrasts between love and sexuality, the better to draw out the keen distinction between love and what we call genital pleasure. By this process we shall have a more precise idea of how far they depend upon one another, and of how far they are mutually independent. This sort of precision will help teachers to guard the sacred and human meaning of the word "love".

A Contrast of Origin

To begin with, we have the first stirrings of love and the sexual instinct in adolescents. It is a general principle that the sexual instinct in young men makes itself felt before the feeling of love. Every investigation made on the subject has shown that a young man is hard-put to get out of himself, to escape from the temptations and urge to auto-eroticism and narcissism. In other words, his battle is to break the chains put round him by his unconscious self-love, to free himself for the altruism of real love. Frequently some encounter with genuine love brings him out of himself and, even, helps him get rid of some personal faults.

In young women, on the other hand, the sexual instinct usually remains latent for a longer time. They feel impelled to love before they are fully aware of desire. This is why, incidentally, young girls who have not been sufficiently instructed frequently misunderstand or misinterpret the psychology of young men.

Psychologists tell us that, normally, it is not until a girl is married that sexual desire really begins to blossom forth. Until then, it is more or less dormant and unspecified, and it is marriage only which brings it to its full strength and resonance.

We have a good manifestation of the difference between love and sexuality in these parallel, but not identical, patterns of development.

*   *   *

The contrast is even more marked if we analyze the peculiar traits of love and the sexual drive.

A Contrast of Duration

Love is a human experience that grows and endures, linking the partners for life. They must love each other for life. They want to love each other always and for ever. Love should grow and develop with them.

The physical act of love, on the other hand, shows an entirely different nature. It lasts a relatively short time and, for various reasons, it sometimes cannot take place for a long time. Once the sexual instinct has been satisfied, it loses its urgency and even, with old age, finishes by weakening and dying. It is the slave of time. A home built on the sexual instinct is threatened by the simple fact that time passes and the husband and wife will change with passing

time. The home's foundation today will disappear tomorrow; what will marital and familial fidelity have to
depend upon?

Contrariwise, love conquers time and grows stronger as
time passes. In his *Essay on Human Love*[1] Jean Guitton
writes:

> It is true that marriage is the fruit of love; it is still
> more true that love is the fruit of marriage. And the art
> of loving is not in the least merely a gathering of the
> fruits of voluptuousness as Ovid, Catullus and the liber-
> tine tradition supposed; it is rather the science of making
> the fleeting love of youth endure and multiply through-
> out the course of a long human life. In spite of the deep
> identity which the vow of fidelity expresses, like every
> normal feeling, love is, in fact, a state of continual trans-
> formation.

That is exactly the point; love is a victory over time and
even over death. In its own way, it is a foretaste of eternity.
Permanence and fidelity are essential parts of its vital fabric.
Zundel, with extraordinary depth, has said: "Fidelity is
the increasingly free choice granted by an increasingly
strong love."

By now this contrast must be clear.

A Contrast of Altruism

No one, of course, should distinguish between the sexual
instinct and love to the point of making the one a function
of the animal part of man's nature and the other a function
of his spiritual side. Doing this would be forgetting that
man is a unity and that even the animal in him is shot
through with his spirituality. Still, the fact remains that
man's sexual instinct is rooted in the lower part of his nature
and is influenced by it.

[1] London and New York, 1951, p. 89.

In itself, the sexual instinct is self-centred, looks out for its own interests and rather tends to subjugate other people to its own ends, without respect for their dignity and independence as persons. It makes people means to ends, to the point of enslaving them and holding them captive.

Love, on the other hand, is basically a respect for another as a person; love cannot do without respect any more than the lungs can do without air. As the poet wrote, "I could not love thee, dear, so much, loved I not honour more".

Love is never the combined selfishness of two people nor one's desire to lord it over the other. Nor is it ever the "selfishness capable of all unselfishness" which it has been called. Love offers and is not possessive, or, at least, its possession is mixed with a gift of self. Love is a promise of giving in proportion to its growth and maturity, whereas desire, using the subterfuge of emotion and affection, gives very little. Love has to distinguish itself from desire to be thoroughly human and to grow deep in the soul. Because there is so much selfishness involved in the "politics of love", there is so little real love in many families. Reducing love to a search for sexual pleasure is weakening it.

The Church, consequently, insists not principally because she is anxious about her own doctrine, but to safeguard the true nature of love and its perquisites, that the first rule of love is honesty with oneself, respect for one's nature. The Church's quarrel with modern literature is not that it is always preaching love and about love, but that it does not know what love really is, has not even set foot in the kingdom of true love, and is so far from realizing the true nobility of the human condition that it is pitiful.

In some cases, love and genital pleasure are so distinct that they are completely dissociated. To begin at the bottom, they are farthest from one another in debauchery. Prostitution, the diametric opposition of love, is a perfect example to show that love and physical satisfaction are two distinct

things. In a report on the role played by men in prostitution,
Dr René Biot wrote:

> The whole problem lies in finding out whether men's
> sexuality is the same force that drives animals to copulate,
> or if it is essentially modified by the same spiritual factor
> that makes his nature different from the animals'.

If the first hypothesis is true, there is nothing to say
that a man cannot look here or there for a partner, and
find one on the streets or in special houses. But if, as we
wholeheartedly believe, human sexuality is necessary
incorporated into a far more complex unity, if even
human nature demands that it must be spiritualized by
love, then any act of love which a man indulges in outside the single and ultimate love of marriage is not only
weakness, which makes him morally less a man, but a
caricature of genuine human sexuality.

Therein lies the root evil of prostitution. It brings man
to the point where he forgets that his sexual power should
not be divorced from love. It is not a question simply of
affection—that could still be on the level of feeling—but
of the strong and definite level of love, with all the word
implies. A house of prostitution is a neverending, concrete statement of the dissociation of love and sexuality.

That is the contrast as it appears on its lowest level; it
will be well to examine the same contrast on its highest
plane.

Ultimately, the dissociation of love and genital pleasure
will be most strongly felt in heaven. We all know the passage
in the Gospels where our Lord says that there will be no
marriage in heaven: *neque nubent, neque nubentur*. Does
this mean that married couples will no longer love one another
in heaven? No; though their love will no longer be sexual,
it will be the same as on earth. Or, rather, it will be greater
and grow to complete perfection. In its new situation and

new surroundings, it will show a new and keener delicacy and sensitivity. The Beatific Vision, heaven's essential joy, will have a corporal resonance and will shine in the glorified bodies of the just. At the resurrection, bodies will be joined with souls with as much suppleness as power. The new powers the body receives will be nothing more than the manifestation of the sensible acceptance of spiritual perquisites; matter will, finally, be obedient to the spirit, not suppressed but liberated. Though the marriage act will no longer have its principal reason for existence in heaven, married love will not be without sensible manifestation there.

To conclude, let us take a look at the best example of all this. The marriage of our Lady and St Joseph was the most perfect example of this disjunction. Thank heaven that we are no longer given pictures and statues of St Joseph in which he looks like a wizened old man, more like a shadow than a man. More and more, we have come to see in this marriage the portrayal of love at its highest and best, though it was, of course, a marriage of complete continence. Catholic theologians do well to insist on the genuine character of this marriage where one sees, in a unique union, virginal tenderness joined with deep love. The fact that the marriage was founded on continence did not lessen the love Mary and Joseph had for one another, but brought the potentialities of their married love to their highest peak.

Some spiritual authors discuss this subject and say that because our Lady and St Joseph were continent their marriage was more "pure" than others. This sort of language implies an idea which is unacceptable and, at bottom, heretical. It leads people to believe that the marriage act is imperfect, or very much like a sin. When the act is performed by a husband and wife who love God and love one another rightly, it is as pure as any other gesture of love. The excellence of our Lady's and St Joseph's continence did

4

not lie in some sort of superior "purity", but in their loyalty to a higher vocation.

It is a fine example of the principle that not simple celibacy, but celibacy consecrated to God, is higher than the married state, because the consecration supposes a more manifold giving of oneself to others and because its consequent liberty makes one free to be at the disposal of more families than one. It is not a question of contempt for one state, but of preference for another, nor does it mean concern for self but loving solicitude for the whole world. Freely chosen continence is the paradoxical counter to married love in that its object is the whole world. The marriage of Mary and Joseph brings us to the point where we re-think our ideas on married love, giving it a Christian perspective and dimension.

This brief outline makes it clear to what extent the modern world is confused about the foundation of real love and how, consequently, true love is constantly compromised. Having covered this field and seen how sexual control is essentially a part of genuine love, we may now more easily take up the rules for an instruction capable of strengthening that control.

Chapter IV

THE ABSOLUTE NEED FOR SEXUAL CONTROL

Continuity of Life

EVERY man is obliged to practise self-control in sexual matters before he is married, after marriage or if he never marries. Marriage is not a new state in which control is no longer necessary. It may provide new and different ways and occasions, but does not do away with control completely. Too many people think that an unmarried person's obligations to be chaste end with marriage, and that it is a sort of reversal of legislation, so that what has been forbidden suddenly becomes allowed. They think, in a word, that marriage is "sinning without sinning", "legalized sin". It is shocking to see that, in many people's subconscious minds, there is a break in continuity between the two states of life—such muddled and morally confused thinking! It is almost as though they held as presupposed that only unmarried people can be "perfectly chaste". They are surprised when anyone talks of marital chastity because there seems to be a contradiction of terms in the expression. Pius XI, however, used the very idea in his great encyclical letter on marriage, *Casti Connubii,* "The Chaste Marriage Union." Putting the two ideas together is perfectly normal and when we are astonished at the usage it is because we forget the two faces, as it were, of chastity, chastity in marriage and chastity outside marriage.

A celibate's sexual life is ordered by chastity's forbidding him anything contrary to the virtue. In marriage, chastity orders the couple's sexual life by placing it in the service of conjugal love. This distinction can never be repeated too often to those people who imagine that marriage puts an end once and for all to pre-marital obligations, almost as though marriage gave a "Drive on!" signal to the sex instinct.

Things are never as simple as that and, in reality, there are certain obligations to self-denial which are operative after marriage as well as before although, as we shall soon see, there is an added, common sexual control in marriage which is just as important and necessary, though in a different set of circumstances and needs, as individual, personal control.

Here, then, is a starting-point for our discussion of the need for sexual control and our enquiry into the ways and means to help more people achieve that goal. Of course, when we say "sexual control" we imply self-control simply. Whatever can help a person gain self-control in general can help him gain sexual mastery of himself. For Christians, self-control is the work of the will and grace, of a will sustained and vivified by grace and strengthened by frequenting the Sacraments. At the bottom of this strong and faithful training is the Christian's idea of life; the quest for control leads one to a full appreciation of life and enables one to live as an integrated Christian. On the other hand, although sexual control is implied in the general notion of self-control, it nevertheless has its own specific laws which suppose and complement the general principles, and it is this aspect of the problem we shall concentrate on here, the more so since the Church demands uncompromising sexual control from men and considers this not only as redounding to her glory, but also as a responsibility which must be accepted and borne.

We have no right to rest content with placing upon men an obligation in God's name without at the same time telling them how to meet the obligation and without encouraging them at every step along the way. For instance: when the Church says that people must go to Mass on Sunday, she undertakes to build churches for them which are conveniently situated and makes the churches comfortable to accommodate the faithful, who may have made sacrifices to fulfil their obligation. Logically, therefore, we must make God's will known here and help others fulfil it precisely. The sins of omission and laziness of those who, for whatever reason, have the job of giving sex instruction will weigh heavier on the last day than the sins of the men and women who were never sufficiently instructed to meet their obligations. In the second part of this book, we shall indicate specifically the degree of responsibility various persons have in this question relative to their respective functions. But first we must point out a defect in this chain of responsibility which is, unfortunately, all too noticeable.

A Gap to be Filled

The lack we are talking about is the absence of adequate and serious preparation for marriage. Granted that recent years have seen much important work in this field, work which one can only applaud; granted also that there are many priests who have taken this need to heart and are bravely trying to fill the gap. But one look at the overall picture and the wide range of individual needs only leads us to feel that we are doing practically nothing.

To sharpen the idea of how great the need is, compare the instruction given before other Sacraments are received with what is given before marriage.

Before first Holy Communion, candidates are very wisely instructed in the catechism; where the custom of solemn Communion is observed, the preparation lasts two years and the requisite familiarity with doctrine is high and exacting.

There is an even more striking contrast when we come to the priesthood. Two years of philosophy are demanded, and four years of theology. It all adds up to an impressive amount of prayer, study, hard work and precise preparation.

Contrariwise, preparation for marriage is often offhand or completely passed over. In the vast majority of cases, people marry with no preparation at all. Marriage seems to be considered as something which will look after itself, an everyday, commonplace business. Because they must, the engaged couple visit their parish priest some days before their wedding day. They come to the meeting with their minds preoccupied with other things and last-minute preparations. They have been told that they must come, and so they do, as though it were only a formality. For what it is worth, they reply to a list of questions and leave after—if they are of the more fortunate few—having been given a short talk on the meaning of marriage, a talk which all too often is very brief.

How does this lack of preparation for marriage correspond with the Church's doctrine on the Sacrament? She teaches that the Sacrament of Matrimony joins husband and wife together in a lifelong, unbreakable union; that it excludes the possibility of divorce and remarriage, no matter what; that its first end is the procreation of children and any frustration of that end is mortally sinful; that it involves not only the future lives of the couple, but the founding of a family, service to society, and ensuring souls for heaven.

Too often, unfortunately, there is a marked contrast between the sacred nature of the marriage alliance and the light, sometimes frivolous, way that many couples undertake this sacred contract.

We absolutely must make up for this lack in pastoral activity and bring all our efforts to bear on solving this gigantic problem. No one pretends that it will be an easy job, but is that any reason for not even trying? Some dioceses in the United States insist that engaged couples attend marriage preparatory conferences and discussions for a few weeks before their marriage. This is a step in the right direction. Young people have already shown interest in and gratitude for the few sketchy attempts made to revive esteem for the seriousness of the engagement period and to prepare engaged couples for marriage by retreats or days of recollection. A small, well-instructed group of people realize how important and necessary these things are, but many, many people have still to appreciate them. We cannot forget the many who hunger and thirst in a spiritual desert but do not even know how bad their condition is. Further, these people who need sexual instruction are not all engaged couples. Some of them will never marry, or will marry late in life; others are already married but are beset by hundreds of problems and hunger after God's word and His grace. These are the people who are in crying need of instruction.

Conditions for Success

Later, we shall examine the ways to consolidate efficiently the various attempts being made to answer this need. For now, however, our discussion will be of the means to achieving a successful instruction towards sexual control on the personal level.

At the outset, we have to repeat and underline what we have already said, that the need for control does not originate only from what the Church expects, but arises primarily from the very nature and dynamic of love itself. This is why we brought out the basic confusion that exists, and distinguished between sexual instinct and love.

The Church certainly does not deprecate love, but rather respects it and would like to see it develop as it must. But only a long educative process can bring this about; if love should be the dynamic core and motivating force of instinct, then people have to be taught how to grow in love and how to penetrate their natural instinct with the force of love. Their maturity in this respect is an index of how strong their sexual control is, but their control needs to be directed and led on to its terminal perfection. If this training is to be successful, Christians have to be shown that the task is simultaneously natural and supernatural. They have to be shown that whatever means they have on both these levels must be co-ordinated to reaching this single goal.

A Supernatural Task

To begin with, we have human nature as we know it: looking at it with the supernatural realism of faith, we see that the natural order, as such, does not exist. In fact, there is only the supernatural order, within whose context nature operates. By reason of the supernatural order, God did not only create men, He is also their Father, and we are not merely creatures but God's children. We have been invited to share the divine life itself, and God makes this invitation and actually brings us to the sharing. In the Sacraments we have God's way of making man holy, helping him to live and strengthening him for the supernatural life which, indeed, begins with baptism. Wanting to live as a complete and integral human being without grace is utopianism; the Christian knows that a strictly human life is really sub-human, and less than he was made for. It leads him off the path to complete life. The man who wants to make a full response to his vocation as human has to be saturated with the supernatural.

Sexual control is certainly the soul's mastery of the body, but it is first God's mastery of the soul. God's control of the soul and the soul's control of the body are the harmonious human combine at the root of the divine creative thought.

Whatever reinforces God's direction of the soul strengthens the soul's control of the body, and any type of penetrating education must build itself on that principle.

Original Sin

Human nature, plunged though it is into the super-natural order, is not intact. We must always remember this fact because to forget it would be to base education on a false premise. We still feel the bad effects of Rousseau and modern literature and even some modern Christians' attitudes have been invaded by Pelagianism, that heretical doctrine that nature is self-sufficient to observe the natural law and does not need the help of grace. Christians, however, believe in Original Sin, which Pascal called a mystery which makes the mystery of our human condition less mysterious. They believe that, without grace, we could not even persist in complete reverence for the natural law, far less in our sexuality than in any other activities.

Implicit in instruction in self-control, consequently, is a renewed recourse to prayer and grace at every stage and, for faithful children of the Church, a strong sacramental life. No matter how weak our nature is, it remains true that God gives us His grace, abundantly and more, if we ask for it humbly in prayer. When St Paul complained that the had suffered so much, God answered, "My grace is enough for you". It is enough for every man, if he will only remember how much he needs it and put out his hand to beg it from his Saviour. Modern men barely realize how much they need redemption and salvation!

Frequenting the Sacraments

Three Sacraments are especially operative in super-natural education to sexual control.

The Eucharist, which the liturgy calls a "safeguard of body and soul", is a pledge of the final resurrection and triumph of the soul over matter. It is the particular Sacrament for spiritual and bodily harmony and control.

Penance paves the way to Holy Communion but it also leads us to greater purity of soul and more complete spiritual development. In addition, it provides for priests' help in instructing and guiding Christian consciences.

Matrimony daily strengthens and energizes married life as it goes on by an influx of God's love, "ever ancient but always new". In *Casti Connubii*, Pius XI recalled, after Bellarmine, that the Sacrament of Matrimony is like the Sacrament of the Eucharist which is not only "a Sacrament at the moment of its accomplishment, in the Consecration, but remains such for as long as the sacred species endure". It is, of course, an analogy which cannot be pushed too far since Matrimony, strictly speaking, is a Sacrament in the passing act of mutual consent and contract.

It is so true, however, that, as Pius XI said, marriage is "a Sacrament whose efficacy lasts for ever", since it seals the marriage bond, the society which husband and wife compose and constitute. When people marry, they do not enjoy the reality of the Sacrament for the short time of the actual wedding ceremony, but for ever, in the power of the Sacrament which unites them "for better or worse". The grace of the Sacrament vivifies from within every gesture of goodwill as well as every expression of loving tenderness. It changes natural human love into supernatural love and charity and brings it about that the couple do not love one another merely with their human hearts—necessarily weak and fragile—but, indeed, with God's heart, at work within them.

The grace of the Sacrament does more than purify by doing away with mere carnality; it lends a quality to human love which is beyond its natural powers, it conquers without humiliating. Love's supernatural elevation is not a weakening or lessening, but a healing restoration.

With regard to the sacrament of marriage, we may use Péguy's dynamic words :

Grace will soar high above nature, but nature will not be tricked and humbled.

A temperature will rise, but not because the freezing point has been lowered.

So eternal values will rise far above temporal ones without any abatement of the latter.

The grace of the Sacrament joins the couple in the redemptive mystery of Christ and leads them on to a deepening and ever richer participation in His sacrifice. It is a preparation for self-sacrifice based on the sacrifice of the altar.

Finally, this grace consecrates the couple as they carry out their peculiar role in the Church: once a home is established it becomes, without ceasing in any way to be a home and precisely because it is a home, a household of charity, a cell of the Church, a source of apostolicity. As Mr Eliot says, "Home is where one starts from."

We must not forget that, if a Christian home is to develop and reach its potential harmony, it should not be isolated and closed in on itself. It has to be wide open to the demands and appeals of the world and the Church. A home's social and apostolic involvement is a necessary part of Christian life, none of whose parts and aspects can be disregarded lightly.

Order builds up order, life feeds life, and love for God and men is harmonized and directed by that deep love which joins husband and wife. There is an indestructible link between self-control and helping others while forgetting self. No one can hope to integrate a human nature disorganized by Original Sin without depending on supernatural grace's great supply of strength. Trying to do it otherwise is basically unrealistic and can only end in failure.

A Natural Task

Although human nature is weakened, it is not, however, basically corrupt. It is not true that men are devoted to sin, or that they are only semi-adult or semi-responsible. Just because human nature is deeply wounded does not mean that it has lost its essential powers. The same realistic attitude which leads us to depend on vitalizing and healing grace encourages us to believe in man's potential and his hidden dynamism. This is the source of that confidence in men's capabilities which any sexual education must start with.

This confidence is nothing more than a reasonable, motivated and enduring faith that self-control can be achieved.

After the American Civil War, Admiral Dupont was called in to explain to Admiral Farragut why he had not been able to lead his ships into Charleston harbour. Once he had listened to Dupont, Farragut said, "There is another reason: you didn't *believe* you could do it." This little story gives a striking example of what we are talking about.

Believing that one can succeed is essential to success; indeed, it is part of success. In this field we need the same sort of confidence we need to drive a car or to swim, where self-confidence is the key to success. It controls the selection and efficiency of technique and is itself the highest and most powerful technique. Many beginners at driving or swimming have given up because they were convinced they could not "do it".

In the sexual field, discouragement and feelings of the "impossibility" of the task beset us from within ourselves, from motives we may not even be aware of. We have to revive our confidence and not let ourselves be led astray by so much modern literature which makes it an unwavering rule that we can never throw off our sexual instinct's domination. By doing this, we implicitly admit that sin is inevitable, or even does not exist, and we thereby give sin the upper hand. Satan is the only one who benefits at all—and he gains everything in this case—from his pessimistic attitude.

But it is not only pessimistic, it is not even a realistic view. Nobody is any more naïve about how strong the sexual instinct is than a swimmer underestimates the force of the sea he is in. But, in both cases, much of the resistance offered depends to a certain extent on the person's frame of mind and attitude.

The sexual instinct is surely one of the strongest but it loses much of its power if it is left alone and not stimulated. What makes the sexual instinct so strong and almost exaggerated today is the society we live in. The combined onslaught of films, pictures, radio programmes, literature, television and the rest make what is essentially a normal instinct almost an obsession. But the obsessive quality comes from all this artificial stimulation. The sexual instinct, when left to itself, is far less hectic than modern civilization would lead one to think.

Modern Man and Self-Conquest

We have, then, to keep the double aspect of natural and supernatural in mind as we continue the investigation of the aid modern science can give us in acquiring self-control sexually. Without overestimating it or making it some quick and easy method to success, we have, at the same time, to realize the practical and concrete help it can give, within a limited field, towards helping men conquer and control themselves.

Science has made extraordinary advances in conquering the world. It has gone right into the core of matter to liberate nuclear energy; it has crisscrossed space with "sputniks", "luniks", and other rockets; it has explored unknown lands and investigated the deepest seas. Scientists have been discovering new and quick weapons against disease and death. Surprisingly, however, they have achieved comparatively little towards understanding man's depths and potentialities, and have still not discovered how to help him to self-mastery and control.

Alexis Carrel spoke of "man the unknown". We are still on the far side of discovering the secret of self-control, of man's mastering himself and, especially, his sexual instincts. Without such control no man is truly integrated. More than in other areas of life, the Socratic "Know thyself" sets a particularly thorny problem.

Science may still be groping, but at least it is going in the right direction. Every day more and more psychologists underline the influence of the soul on the body, of the psychic on the physical. In the world of medicine, the application of this interaction has had some remarkably successful effects. The influence of the moral nature on health and the dependence of functional disorders on mental conditions has long been realized. It is more than ever understood today. Wittkower writes: "The alleged physiological impulsion, strange as it may seem, plays a minor part in most cases of sexual promiscuity, as thirst has little relation with chronic alcoholism."

Psychoanalysis too has shown how important a part the factors of introversion and egocentric stagnation play in the matter. Science deviates more and more from the claim of irresistible impulses to which profligacy, under the guise of "free love", formerly appealed in self-justification.

At present, in biology, genital reflexes are classed in the category of those which can be more easily modified through a deliberate and progressive training.

A relatively new science, psychophysiology, has widened even further the field of those conquests of the spirit over the body. Pius XII did not hesitate to allude to it and to release that science and the discoveries due to it from the cloak of philosophy in which some of its promoters earthed it.

The progress of science, and in particular of biological science, has shown the theory of a certain materialistic and mechanical condition to be out of date. Pavlov and others have thrown new light on the relations of the brain and the mental processes and have defined more accurately the laws governing the interaction of the different innate and conditioned reflexes. This science of reflexes helped create a psychology of conscience whose direction lies towards showing how man is active in gradually gaining control of his destiny, contrary to the psychology which too strongly insisted on man's passivity and the combined effect on him of heredity and environment. Whatever the philosophic setting of these various new psychologies and their discoveries, they are leading to a fuller appreciation of the spiritual side of man's nature, an appreciation which can only be liberating.

Modern psychophysiologists now insist on certain postulates which of their nature stimulate the struggle for sexual mastery. In the first place, they lay down that man's sexuality, unlike an animal's which is closely linked to the automatic, is much more pliable and more widely susceptible to training than was previously thought. A human being's sex lies more in his brain than in his hormones, and the brain has a wider control and a great power of direction than most people think. Man's instincts are not like an animal's, but are physiological reflexes based on his humanity. Human sexuality is brain-centred and consequently depends on the reflexes' controlling centre. Human sexual behaviour does not depend on innate reactions, but largely upon acquired reactions, conditioned reflexes and habit received and assimilated from environment. By the means of painless childbirth, for instance, the study of reflexes has demonstrated that there is a deeper control over reflexes than people commonly believed. Though the

physiology of pain is different from the physiology of pleasure, still it would be worthwhile to use the analogy between
them to conduct parallel if not identical research.

In his book *Maîtrise Sexuelle* (Paris, 1959), Dr. Paul
Chauchard writes :

> An animal can use all its powers as soon as it is fully
> matured, but a man cannot, except insofar as he has
> learned to use his brain. Animals have only to follow
> their instincts, man must devise what he will do; his in-
> stincts are little developed and he can in great measure
> discipline and master them (p. 9).
> ... Unlike animals, who exercise their sexual powers
> perfectly from instinct alone without any training, man
> depends in this area—a sadly neglected truth—entirely
> upon his upbringing (p. 13).
> ... Compared to what happens in animals, once the
> principal sexual control has been transferred to the brain,
> automatic instinctive behaviour lessens.... We would
> say that man's sexual instinct is an instinct in a different
> sense from an animal's.... Practically speaking, all our
> sexual behaviour, except for a few, purely elementary
> reflex reactions, is conditioned reflex. This conditioning
> can be quite extensive.... We may also say that, just as
> we are present to ourselves in our brains, so our sex is in
> our brains.... A thing is only as sexual as it provokes
> the activity of latent sexual structures in the brain and is
> aware of them; if a sensitive impulse or a usually sexual
> thought is accepted by the brain in a non-sexual context,
> then it is no longer cerebrally sexual and loses sexual
> power. (p. 42)[1]

Mental hygiene plays as great a part in sexual control as
other kinds of hygiene.

[1] Cp. also the same author's "Les voies nouvelles de la psychologie",
Revue des Questions scientifiques (20 Jan. 1955), pp. 110-118; "Aspects
neurophysiologiques des conduites humaines", *Ibid.* (20 Jan. 1958),
p. 127.

We give every sign of an irrelevant Puritanism when we belittle these "sorry means and methods" on the pretext of high spirituality. The Church is divine, but she is also human, made for flesh and blood human beings. Further, it is her job to bring this humanity to God.

One of the worst scourges of human nature is alcoholism. We hardly need to labour that point. The damage that alcoholism does where sexual licence is concerned must be emphasized and, with the proper means, fought against and conquered. Some parties and social gatherings are not dangerous so much because both men and women are present but because they drink too much and abuse alcohol to the point where they become artificially stimulated and intoxicated. People can take good example in this matter from athletes who, while "in training", are very moderate in order to ensure success. Also, their regimen of physical exercises is a superb school of self-control and training of the will.

These few considerations far from exhaust the subject. They only give us food for thought on the absolutely essential task of combining natural and supernatural aids and means.

Our next task is to examine the various conditions and circumstances in which this necessary and possible control —possible because necessary—can and should be exercised.

Chapter V

DOUBLE CONTROL IN MARRIAGE

EVERYONE has to have sexual control and no one can begin to develop it too soon. For a married couple, however, it is doubly essential and it has a special marital aspect which needs considering.

The Marriage Union

Any study of marital morality must begin with the initial proposition that the married couple are a unity, a man and woman joined to one another in an indissoluble community. It is essential to understand, respect and realize the importance of this union as the first and original reality of marriage. Instead of thinking of marriage as two people living side by side in a casual, strictly convenient union, we must always think of it in terms of a mutual relationship, of reciprocity, sharing and exchange.

In this way, we soon realize that the marriage act is a living bond, a co-operation in which the couple share whatever responsibility for good or evil there may be. If one of the partners counterfeits this act by frustrating its primary end, the innocent party cannot disclaim any responsibility and purely and simply dissociate himself from his partner. As one modern author puts it: "Though it is true that I haven't committed the other's sin and need not confess it, still, because of the basic acceptance which constitutes communion, we *both* are involved, *one with the other,* in our good or bad conscience". This inter-personal communion makes marriage a new state, liable to its own laws and obligations, and conformable to what we can call the law of conjugality. The same author also has this to say with regard to this unity: "I accuse *us* of my partner's sin, and *we* must do all we can together to leave it behind us". Many, many practical consequences may be drawn from that idea.

There has been too much of an individualist approach to marriage in examining the husband's or the wife's attitude separately and in making the joint responsibilities of marriage nothing more than the sum of both partners' separate obligations. There is no area where individualism is more out of place. Moralists would do well to recall what the Gospels have to say: "What God has joined together, let no man put asunder"!

Masculine individualism, especially, has to be guarded against. No one denies, of course, the wisdom of St Paul's "let wives be submissive to their husbands, as is fitting in the Lord". But this implied supremacy by no means weakens or destroys the radical equality of the married couple, nor their unity.

Because of a complexity of sociological and other factors, the marriage union has not always been sufficiently considered as a unity of two equally dignified people. Sometimes the particular dignity of one or the other has not really been clear. Even St Thomas did not avoid this exaggeratedly masculine—and monastic—viewpoint when, in his commentary on the text of Genesis where it says that God made woman to help man, he puts it down with conviction that, apart from procreation, a man is always better helped by another man than by a woman.[1]

Once anything which can do it radical harm has been overcome, the marital unity should be lived in a positive way, under its many different aspects. Let us consider some of these aspects.

[1] *Summa Theologica*, Ia, q. 98, 2.

Respect for Conjugal Unity on the Physical Plane

The rights and dignity of the marriage union begin on the physical level. A married couple's chastity is conjugal, correlative and interdependent. This means that an essential element of this chastity is genuine love, which is reciprocity and sharing. Beginning here, self-control puts its roots even into the heart of the conjugal union which is entirely an action of mutual self-giving and in which each partner has to direct the deepest parts of himself or herself towards the other, living in rhythm with the other. The resulting, natural, physical pleasure is not, primarily, a satisfaction that each partner achieves for himself but, psychologically, it is a joy which each first gives to the other before experiencing it fully himself. Love and control, then, are present at the outset of the act as well as during its progress.

To be fully experienced physically, this joy needs as much simultaneity as possible. Love should urge each partner to do what he can to make it so. Here, again, one needs self-mastery as well as forgetting oneself and putting aside natural selfishness.

The first step towards conjugal chastity, or sexual control, is taken with the first gesture of true love. Forgetting oneself is not a refinement of love, it is the condition for love's success.

God's first demand of the act of love is that it be based on real love. The "crime of non-love" is behind all the broken marriages. Everyone knows how many of them there are and divorce statistics make their frequency all too clear. What does more harm than anything else to married love is one partner's selfishness—or both partners'. That is where the root of the trouble will be found.

It is not by its intensity but by its lack of depth that sexual pleasure is debased. This idea is so true that St Thomas did not hesitate to say that, in God's first plan for men, before Original Sin, this pleasure would have been even greater because it was more ordered, more filled with love.

When we discuss married love, we must not confuse purity and renunciation. Purity does not mean loving less, but loving more deeply. "People never love too much," someone wrote, "they either love badly or not enough."

Nor must we dissociate love from instinct in the marriage act; doing this would be mutilating it, robbing it of its dignity and genuine humanity. The point is not to repudiate the physical side of married love; but rather to get the physical aspect imbued with the spiritual and with natural and supernatural love. The Church's condemnation applies only to any act of love which is somehow unnatural, the contradiction of love. She does not want the act of married love to be performed without that dignifying affection which should motivate it and whose demonstration, symbol and sign it should be.

A physical act of love which does not begin in the soul is a living lie, an act of treason, like Judas' kiss. It is degrading and brings on a separation between the couple's souls. The material side of love has to be activated by the spiritual and love's physical gestures should be motivated and vivified by love itself. Seeking sensation for its own sake, apart from love, means that man never really gets out of himself; it means limiting him to a part only of what he really is and giving a dignity to this part that it really has no right to. It means contemning man's real dignity by destroying the unity of the human composite. There is nothing unworthy in the physical act of love itself, but it becomes unworthy as soon as it loses its spiritual dynamism, and its true meaning and reason for existence. That is the Church's doctrine. She repudiates Jansenism and Manichaeism and, by leading men to self-control, helps them save themselves from themselves and obliges them never to give up the fight.

Jean Lacroix says this very well in his fine book *Force et faiblesse de la famille* (Paris) :

> What should be most guarded against in man is not instinct nor reason but his "exclusivism", as it were; and reason divorced from instinctive vitality is just as dangerous as instinct which has not been incorporated into a system of desires and rational balance. Sexuality is dangerous only when it is isolated; when it is flooded with tenderness and love it is always good. The sexual act is integrated into a man's personality to the extent that he has humanized his whole being. It is, on the other hand, dehumanized just as much as a man allows a dichotomy between his reason and his instinct. Sexuality is in no wise bad, but isolating the sexual function, and tearing it out of its personal context and reducing it to animal sexuality, contrary to human destiny, this is bad. That specious love which is interested in possession only is immorality, pure and simple. (pp. 97-98)

It might be worth while to use this law of conjugality to shed light on some cases of conscience and consider, or review, their more or less classic solutions.

One example is conjugal continence. In some instances it is necessary for a longer or shorter length of time. The whole problem lies in knowing how to practise it concretely and what means to use. Too many young married couples think it means a choice between all or nothing and that they have to live "as brother and sister". They feel that they cannot live this way and soon weaken, eventually to fall into sin. But they should be told that there is another way open to them, a way which is easier and has helped many couples remain faithful to God. It takes an effort, it is true, but it is practicable.

Living as "brother and sister" is more than some couples with good intentions are capable of. Since it involves, by definition, a case of a couple lawfully joined in marriage, the phrase is inadequate. In its own way, it implies a mis-interpretation of the law of conjugality we have been stress-ing. Marriage is not a bachelor and a spinster living to-gether, but a husband and wife. If both partners agree and are motivated by a spirit of renunciation, then, of course, they can choose the more or less radical solution of separa-tion just as, in some very rare and exceptional cases, couples renounce their marriage rights for a very lofty motive deriving from a devotion to social or apostolic work. But this solution is not the normal or usual one.

Ordinarily, conjugal continence means that the husband and wife may use every legitimate means of expressing their love physically without, however, going as far as the act's ordinary conclusion.

Another example is a wife's permitted passivity in the case where her husband indulges in onanistic practices. The problem is all too unfortunately well known and frequent. What should a woman do, what may she allow to be done, if she is sure that her husband will not let the marriage act come to its natural term? Moralists very correctly distin-guish between a case where the husband uses a contra-ceptive device from the start and a case where, after a normal beginning, he interrupts the act.

In the first case, no moralist could sanction this be-haviour without contravening the formal teaching of the Church; in the second case, the classic reply permits the wife, in order to avoid a greater evil, to remain passive once she has tried to dissuade her husband from the sinful practice.

This tolerant opinion is common and, we say this to forestall any uneasiness of conscience, one has the right to follow the opinion of recognized moralists. On the other hand, I should like to see moralists examine the question once more, this time in the light of the principle of con-jugality.

A survey was made among a large number of wives who were practising Catholics. They were of good judgment and by no means scrupulous, but the survey showed that this permitted, moral distinction was repugnant to them. Just because they have been allowed to shut themselves away in passivity does not mean that they were left without uneasiness. And the greater this disquiet, the more careful we must be to protect their interests.

They are the more offended by this moral "dualism" because the passivity in question implies a minimum of active co-operation. Even the fact that they protest, as they are obliged to, is somewhat idealistic, they feel. It seems to them that this permitted passivity is a kind of moralistic trickery; they understand that one may, in case of serious, imminent danger, be resigned and passive, and that this solution can be applied to other serious situations. But they have the vaguely defined feeling that this "condescension" weakens their moral resistance and certainly does not encourage Christian generosity or peace. They know they are not sinning mortally, but they are unanimous in saying that the solution seems to them to be spiritual mediocrity.

Respect for Conjugal Unity on the Spiritual Plane

Marriage is physical communion, but it is still more a communion of soul and life. Man is an entity, and the struggle for sexual control and love's full development must begin deep in the core of this wholeness.

A marriage which begins without perfect spiritual communion is already under a very serious handicap. This is especially true in the case of mixed marriages and even truer when non-believers marry. Obviously, a marriage between people of different religions can be humanly happy, but the risk that it will not be is very great. The Church does not show hesitation and even fear about these unions without good reason. She insists on guarantees that the Catholic partner will be able to continue his or her religious duties and that the children of the marriage will be raised as Catholics. This is, of course, an absolute minimum, and surely it is clear that it is a minimum only?

Differences in ideas and religious convictions are bound to have many repercussions which extend beyond the area of religious practice alone. It is not enough to go to Mass on Sunday and have one's children baptized. Religion, like man, is also an integral thing and it should penetrate life completely, in all its personal, family and social aspects. How can a couple share life's joys and sorrows if they do not both look at their daily life together in the same light and with the same scale of values? How can they both observe the same discipline of conjugal morality if all they really have in common is their life together? There is no getting away from all the problems which will arise: what should their attitude be towards birth control, forbidden by the Church and accepted so widely outside the Church? How will they approach the business of contraceptive practices? What will be a sin for one of them will not be sinful for the other. What about the future, when they have to raise their children together and the children, as soon as they have grown up, will be torn between their father and their mother, forced into making a very painful choice? No one should be surprised to realize that because of these conditions mixed marriages are one of the greatest causes of loss of faith.

Many Catholics find it difficult to understand the Church's reserve towards these marriages. What seems like harshness, however, is really a maternal anxiety for her children who are not only putting themselves in a position where they can lose their faith, but who are also jeopardizing their love because, at its very roots, it is without the communion which means life or death to a home.

Respect for Conjugal Unity in Everyday Life

The law of conjugality applies to more than spiritual and physical harmony in the marriage union. It is a law governing the whole life of a Christian family. It is useless to dream of establishing a happy home without developing this harmony in a family's everyday life.

Love is not simply an isolated act; it is the product of two lives being lived as one. Its whole meaning is tied up in the words of a husband who refers to his wife as "my life's companion". Love grows as days pass and circumstances change. Everything is important to it, especially the many trifles which add up to family happiness. One of its results is a happy and Christian married life; it slips into a context of life and is strengthened by mutual sacrifice, self-forgetfulness, generosity. Actually, these virtues cannot even grow in a baptized soul except in a supernatural atmosphere. They need all the strength they can get from the Sacraments in order to be fed, purified and consolidated. Every deliberate sin makes home-life a little weaker, while every grace accepted and used makes it more robust and better developed.

Since man is a unit, even his non-sexual behaviour is seriously important to his remaining chaste. The obligation to be chaste is one of a set of obligations, all of which must be met. Like men, the virtues too are clannish. Moderation in eating and drinking, controlling one's temper or natural selfishness, controlling one's eyes, all these help to better self-control in married life. On the other hand, however, giving free rein to one's imagination in reading, watching television, films or stage plays can be the first step to a moral lapse. Everything is applicable and everything builds or destroys an atmosphere of chastity. This is all the more reason to consider an act of weakness not merely as it is in itself but as it applies to the whole tenor of one's life.

If a man loyally lives for God and other people, if he

dedicates himself to serving an ideal, if he seriously tries to do good every day, the reasonable presumption is that a lapse will not be entirely deliberate. Circumstances help us to judge events. The best guarantee that a man will remain loyal to his ideals during a passing temptation is his loyalty to those ideals in everyday life.

Modern psychology has successfully combated that psychological atomism which tended to break up life into seconds and judge these instances in isolation from the rest of life. Science has now learned to situate every isolated reaction in relation to life's totality and to judge it in that context. Life is a unit, and isolating one bit of life is misunderstanding reality and setting up false problems. It is the same with regard to moral life, where context is a basic factor. God does not judge one or two instants of a man's life, but a whole life; He listens, as it were, to sentences, not isolated syllables.

Consequently, the obligation to chastity must be seen in relation to other obligations. It is neither the most important nor, indeed, the only obligation. Charity remains Christ's great commandment and charity between husband and wife must combine with their obligation to be chaste and accommodate itself to that obligation. Neither can be sacrificed to the other. An equation is not solved by eliminating the factors but by bringing them into harmony with one another. Harmonizing one's obligations is a delicate task, of course, but it is no less necessary because delicate. Husband and wife are obliged to love one another and to give one another physical demonstration of this love, even if, for the time being, they happen to be living continently. This is a delicate balance, but grace can bolster up the effort to sexual control and help it to work itself out while fidelity to God is preserved.

We must never lose sight of the law of simultaneous obligations. One of Claudel's characters says, "I love things that exist together." We have to love and respect God's laws in all their diversity. It is a mistake to discuss the sixth commandment as though it had no relation to the other nine. We have to be charitable, just and chaste, all at the same time and together. All our obligations are implied in one another and are linked to one another. Charity and chastity, for example, go hand in hand and reinforce and complement each other. On this point, we might remind ourselves that we do not want to be like those people of whom Péguy said that "they think they love God because they don't love anyone". Christianity is not fragmentary, but is a complete, cohesive whole. Good is the end-product of integral abundance: *bonum est ex integra causa*. That philosophical maxim may be applied in numerous ways and is worth its weight in gold.

As J.P. and B. Dubois-Dumée say in their book, *Le Couple chrétien* (Paris, 1950):

> People have gradually made impurity the consummate evil, the number one sin. Stealing, hypocrisy, lying, murder, hardness of heart—none of these is anything as bad as impurity.... Sexual morality must be respected, of course, but it is not the whole of morality.... We hide our faces before lust, because of the element of physiological control, but we do not see that we must also take into account the materially uncontrollable elements of impulses to selfishness and pride. Marriage is a whole and to live in marriage properly, just as to judge any fault, one must consider the whole in all its aspects (pp. 143ff).

These ideas sum up very well the double effort at control we have been discussing and, at the same time, give a precise picture of its limits and scope.

Chapter VI

GRADUAL CONTROL

CHASTITY is not a static virtue, acquired once and for all. It is dynamic and is governed by an internal law of growth, and constantly has to resist the effects of Original Sin in us. Normally, self-control is not achieved overnight but gradually. But this is the way with all human perfection; we must always be working to be more just, more honest, more wise and more charitable.

In the same way, husband and wife have to become gradually more chaste. Love should gradually grow into greater control of instinct. But there are periods of tension and of relaxation in this sustained effort towards control. Let us examine the graph of this control's growth and choose one or two instances which are especially important, either because they relate to the couple's future or because they bring up delicate problems of conscience.

An Obstacle to be Overcome

To a great extent, an adult's efforts to achieve complete sexual control of himself will be conditioned by the way he met and dealt with the sexual crisis of his adolescence. This comes down to what his attitude was to masturbation. The urge to a solitary release of spontaneous or provoked sexual tension is the adolescent's principal sexual temptation.

A young person's response to this temptation involves not only his future sexual growth but his intellectual and emotional life and, sometimes, his whole religious orientation. It is no good minimizing the importance of the matter;

it needs a clear look at the entire question. In *The Problem of Onanism* (Cork, 1955), Dr von Gagen, a Catholic authority on the subject, borrows the following chart from Rohleders' statistical study. It gives the results of a series of investigations, each independent of the others, based on the question whether "the person interviewed had practised masturbation at some time in his life". There was no qualification as to when it happened or for how long a time; the fact only was involved. The figures give the percentages of affirmative answers and are preceded by the names of the investigators:

Meirowsky (students)	71.0 per cent
Meirowsky (doctors)	88.7 per cent
Marro	85.0 per cent
Markuse	93.0 per cent
Dr Deutsch (in Budapest)	96.7 per cent
Prof. Duck	90.8 per cent
Dr Dukes, English medical scholar	90-95.0 per cent
Scarley-Springfield (students)	95.3 per cent
Hirschfeld	96.0 per cent
Dr D. Hahn (workmen)	96.0 per cent
Brockmann	99.3 per cent
Joung, American urologist	100.0 per cent
Berger	100.0 per cent
Moraglia	100.0 per cent

We can add to these the two studies made by Rohleders himself, the figure for the first was 85 per cent and, for the second, 96 per cent. The Catholic director of the Centre for Observation at Chevilly, France, reported that he found that "93 per cent of the men questioned had indulged in solitary pleasure, and 87 per cent of these cases took place in adolescence." He concludes by saying these figures are close to the statistics of the American Kinsey Report.

We do not intend to study these figures here, nor go into the conditions under which each investigation was made.

Instead, it will be enough to underline the impressive agreement of the percentages and their indication of how widespread a phenomenon masturbation is. Educators should be encouraged to devote themselves to this problem which is so important and generates so many dramas of conscience.

Modern psychology has shown that masturbation can result from different, very deep anomalies and that it is often a symptom of an underlying pathological condition. Frequently, a "psychological kink" will create tension which a person releases by masturbating. In getting rid of this trouble in the emotional field—it may be a disappointment in love, or loneliness—the real task may lie in bringing the adolescent out of himself and helping him put off the infantilism which this unfortunate practice reveals. A forthright training to help the young person to a greater consciousness of others, a consciousness based on charity and social dedication, will be a great help towards getting him out of himself. It will also leave him open to benefit as much as possible from the help available in prayer and the Sacraments which must be every Christian's court of appeal. It is impossible to imagine that we would not make an effort to give this guidance and instruction but, instead, would leave the adolescent to fight his own battle in the midst of his anguish and confusion. As someone wrote, "Truth alone can clear up a troubled atmosphere because truth has nothing to do with evil, while a false modesty or shame will confuse a basically healthy atmosphere and strengthen an evil by wanting to ignore it."

Without in any way minimizing the objective seriousness of this evil, we should nevertheless take pains to help young people recognize and distinguish clearly between its objective aspect, which presupposes complete knowledge and complete liberty, and its subjective aspect, which will depend on a complex of factors which he must know if he is to free himself. Victory achieved in this matter will one day be a firm base upon which he can build marital sexual control, since it would be a mistake to imagine that marriage in and of itself is a solution to the problem.

The Beginnings of Married Life

We said that chastity is a gradually developing virtue. A growing plant needs special attention. For this reason, then, husband and wife have to work at common control from the very beginning of their marriage.

If young married couples do not voluntarily exercise this control during the first months and years of marriage, they will one day find themselves abruptly shaken by a longer or shorter period of enforced continence, which is bound to arise sooner or later. If, on the other hand, presupposing that they are not troubled by any fear and are ready to accept the consequences of their decision, they limit their love-making according to the woman's periods of fertility or sterility and realize fully what they are doing, they will inevitably develop a better control of themselves because of this progressive training. Far from hindering their love, their control will be a sign of a greater love, greater because more controlled and more directed towards a higher goal. This psychologically relaxed atmosphere will naturally take on the character of a period of sexual education, an exercise in control from which they will learn everything that will one day be necessary and useful.

Practice in continence is essential not only because of the negative consideration that, sooner or later, it will be necessary, but, more positively, because some sort of asceticism is needed for love's vitality. The Jewish people observe an even stricter asceticism in this matter, precisely for self-control and to make greater fertility possible. Speaking to the Commission on Marriage Guidance during the 1959 meeting in Zurich of the International Union of Family

Groups, Rabbi B. J. Gelles of London presented the Jewish position on birth control thus:

> Each month, beginning with the start of the menstrual period, the couple are obliged not to make love for a certain number of days.
>
> This initial obligation to "separateness" offers many benefits to health as well as psychological and moral advantages: it brings the couple a time of physical rest; revives in them a new feeling of attraction, a reagent against the danger of satiety, a constant threat, with its consequent marital lassitude; and, finally, proves how necessary it is to be able to control the demands of the flesh.

The only reason for citing this position here is to show that, among one class of people at least, periodic continence is not considered an unattainable ideal. We can overlook the specifically Jewish obligation to a periodic but complete separation, and still see that there are advantages in a reasonable use of periodic continence, for knowledge's sake, which may include every normal physical intimacy without ending in the marriage act's usual terminal reflex.

Prevention is better than cure. Some marriage problems are so difficult only because the couple are unprepared for them. The problem itself can be solved, but its solution is made temporarily difficult because there has been no psychological preparation for it. Without this gradual education, couples will inevitably be handicapped and whatever self-control home conditions may suddenly impose will have to be met with greater effort and courage.

Complete chastity, which is the effort towards a perfect harmony between body and soul, may not be reached until after some initial successes and failures due in part to the very nature of the effort. These unsure attempts, trials and renewed efforts will be judged primarily on the basis of the good will inspiring them. This does not mean that lapses may not be blameworthy and that one should not deplore them as culpable. But a growing and strengthening effort puts them in their proper perspective in view of the whole campaign. While waiting for complete control, a time of learning which inures the couple to hardships is the best answer to the usual conditions of married life.

An "all or nothing" attitude is not a good solution because it will work for some strong souls but is not the ordinary and normal way. Married couples must be able to translate their love into physical activity and gestures, even though they are obliged to abstain from the final act of love. This conversion is a part of their union, peace and joy. It helps them achieve the secondary ends of marriage, ends which are no less real and imperative because the primary end may, for some reason, be impossible. We do not consider this physical intimacy in its material aspect, which can be diverse and changing, but in its deep inspiration. A symbol is nothing if it is not filled with meaning. A physical gesture has its value from the love it expresses and which is its content, its source of nobility and its only limit.

It can happen that, until the reflexes have been trained, this physical manifestation of love—up to but not including, as we have said, the inseminating reflex or anything that deliberately or directly provokes it—can sometimes, and in passing, bring about a loss of self-control. Here care must be taken to distinguish between what is voluntary and what is the result of surprise, or a real accident. Also, it has to be decided if this is the usual result or if it is rare. Everyone's conscience is the most loyal judge of what is really an act of the will. The best rule for Christians is to lay the matter before a confessor who will help them clear their conscience and, at the same time, point out where the grave fault is and how to continue with confidence in their struggle to control themselves. Without sacrificing any of the intangible principles of morality, these good but tottering wills have to be bolstered up and stimulated to resume their efforts at achieving that indispensable control and to avoid any act whose serious gravity is undeniable. So, it is a question of not being discouraged; with God's grace, success is the outcome of every sustained effort.

Surely it is not necessary to repeat that this hazardous training cannot succeed without an accompanying recourse to prayer and the support of grace through a faithful and strong sacramental life. The best physical exercises are doomed to failure if the human body is not fed properly; health is the result of co-ordinated and integral efforts. Moral health is the same for a Christian, and he should never overlook the strengthening it gets from the supernatural. Grace is not a veneer laid over nature, but runs through it like a thread, vitalizing it from within. A weak body makes gymnastics useless, and a Christian soul cut off from its sources of supernatural strength can never fully develop. With these aids, however, and by their regular and faithful use, this training will be the more valuable.

Love and Faithfulness

Love is not a completely fashioned reality but builds itself on fidelity. Fidelity, in its turn, can only endure and deepen if love remains ruler over instinct, giving it life as the soul does the body and refusing any disintegration or separation. Usually, instinct wears itself out, and quickly. The remedy for this situation, however, is not to accept it and resort to a mechanical repetition of acts of love. It needs a renewal and the soul's increased efforts in love's control of instinct, no matter how love's manifestation may change as years go by. Faithfulness is the result of this growth which is itself the fruit of theological charity's greater and greater victories in a human heart.

A couple may reach that dangerous stage where one of them, threatening to break up the marriage, is on the point of yielding to a temptation. In this case, more than ever, the obligation to Christian fidelity comes into operation. We say "Christian fidelity" because it could too easily happen that a person would try to protect a compromised marriage by recourse to the principle of "the lesser evil" by yielding to his or her partner's onanism.

We have already discussed this point in so far as shared responsibility is concerned. We must remark here that, in the case of infidelity, the end that is desired by passivity cannot be achieved in this way. Fidelity comes from grace, not passion. No one can consent, even materially, to a partner's sin and thereby hope to keep him faithful to the love to which he vowed fidelity before God and men. Sin begets sin; only co-operation with grace can do the work of grace and salvation. Scripture asks, "If the Lord does not guard the city, who will save it?" This applies to that city in miniature which is the Christian home, so beset by danger. Evil does not generate good, and God's work is done in God's way, not otherwise.

How could fidelity, furthermore, result from a moral compromise or concession? No one tries to keep an alcoholic from drinking elsewhere by giving him as much whiskey as he wants at home.

The only way to fight against infidelity is by doubling fidelity to God by prayer and the Sacraments and, at the same time, by building up genuine love for the offending partner. True marital fidelity is a continuous counterpoint of love in marital relations and is fostered not by excitement but by love. Love lends control, self-mastery, fidelity. Physical excitement, by itself and cut off from love, is nothing more than excitement.

Anyone who thinks that love can be safeguarded by allowing instinct free rein is confusing love and instinct. The contrary is true; love safeguards physical union and guarantees its endurance. Divorced from love, instinct is at the mercy of any kind of determinist influence; it is the plaything of whatever is most attractive. By thinking that to give in to human weakness we can thereby ensure a safe future, we actually speed up some sort of break because the remedy which has been suggested or allowed—in the case of onanism—can only make bad come to worse.

Fidelity's rehabilitation cannot result from sin, but from grace only; spiritual death can only bring on more spiritual death. By making it easier for a blameworthy partner to sin, a husband or wife does not facilitate, but hinders, the saving resurgence of conscience.

The love that grows in the soul of a faithful partner is more than human love. More than anything else, it is Christian love, love without bounds made richer by God's own love.

In the sort of case we have been considering, the truly Christian partner has to love the other more and better, and not only with his or her poor, injured human love, but with God's love. Our limited perceptiveness can scarcely begin to measure the broad extent of that great love. When we say that the faithful partner must love even with God's own heart, we mean that the love must be completely not of this world.

God loved and loves men first. St John put down this fact in an unforgettable sentence. God's love is freely given and does not depend on our response. It is obstinately loyal, even if we betray it. God loves, as it were, beyond rhyme or reason, completely forgetting Himself. He loves us despite our blemishes and our betrayals. He is without that hyper-sensitivity which turns in on itself and that susceptibility which can bring on bitterness and aggressiveness. The faithful partner should share this unflagging and enduring love if he or she wants to live up to what God expects in the troubled circumstances and to do everything possible to save the home.

Everyone knows something about these saddening cases
where open or secret infidelity is at work. What can one do
in these circumstances? Humanly speaking, nothing. But
from a Christian point of view, one should re-read our
Lord's injunction about pardoning seventy times seven,
even if it means risking still more misunderstanding, ridi-
cule, quarrelsome ingratitude and even contempt. When
every attempt at saving the marriage seems futile, more
patient and courageous love is needed; it is no good falling
into recriminations and reproaches, but one should love as
the Prodigal Son's father did, who waited for the sinner
to return and loved his son with a love stronger and greater
than the young man's sin.

The unfaithful husband or wife remains God's child, entrusted to the faithful partner's care even if, on earth, they
cannot be reconciled. A Christian is forbidden to have recourse to divorce, which would be still another betrayal. A
mother loves her child no matter what and never divorces
herself from her child. A woman's husband, though he
may be unfaithful, is still, in God's eyes, her firstborn son.
She must continue to love him, just as one loves a sick person, and, in her most secret heart, keep faith with the trust
God has irrevocably placed in her.

This idea is laden with implications of heroism; it is a
wearying burden of sufferings which God invites anyone
threatened with infidelity to accept and bear. It is, however, the way of the Gospels and there is no other way
through tears and pain to deeper peace and joy. It will
bring that peace "which no man can take away" that our
Lord promised to whomever serves Him to the end. At
death it will be easier to understand how such suffering
could help save the one who betrayed love. Someone has
called love "a sentence whose full sense we do not get until
the very last word has been said". When death, and only
death, puts a full stop to a love vowed before God's altar,

then we shall realize the worth of a love that has been sacrificed and crucified but which remains a source of life, victorious over death.

Chapter VII

CONTROL AND FERTILITY

THE full effect of a revolution can only be measured after some time has passed. In 1930, the world-wide press announced that Prof. Ogino, in Japan, and Dr Knaus, in Austria, had independently of one another but almost simultaneously discovered how to determine the fertile and sterile days of a woman's menstrual cycle. After experts had hesitated about the validity of the Ogino-Knaus law, and moralists about the legitimacy of its use, it was enthusiastically received.

The discovery brought a flood of consequences after it. What used to be left to chance was now put under men's control. After a fashion, it put the key to the kingdom of life in men's hands, in most cases at least. Also, while the old choice used to be either indeterminable fertility or complete abstention, there now arose a new problem of conscience: the voluntary use of the periods of fertility and sterility and, even, man's controlling use of the natural rhythm. Previously, the marriage act was very frequently performed blindly, on the spur of the moment perhaps, without any thought of the consequences or of the responsibilities it might engender. Now, science had given man the ability to perform the act more reasonably insofar as he could now take anterior responsibility for any eventual consequences.

Because of this fact, a new moral obligation arose. What had formerly been left to nature's unknown whim, without any influence of human reason, was now, for a Christian,

something to be carried out in God's sight, but an action
which demanded from him a considered choice. Because of
his better knowledge of himself and nature's laws, it was
now up to him to regulate deliberately the relation between
self-control and fertility.

All this brought men to a neater re-thinking of the ends
of marriage so that they could put the obligation to have
children in a sharper focus and examine how to meet it.

Two Complementary Ends

There are two places where Genesis touches on the ends
of marriage. In the first place (1. 26-31), the creation of the
human couple is the crowning work of the six days of creation. There is a deliberate parallelism in the various stages
of creation. It is said of the trees and plants that they bore
"their seed according to their species", and that they bore
"fruit having within it seed". The animals were told, with
God's blessing, to increase their number. Finally, when
Adam and Eve have been created, God tells them to "increase and multiply, and fill the face of the earth". This
first passage in Genesis is filled with the idea of life's trans-
mission through the obligation to perpetuate and develop
the human race.

The second passage (2.7-25) is very different. Adam is
created before woman and God says that "it is not good
for man to be alone", so He decides to make a companion
for Adam, "a helper like himself". Adam recognizes in her
what he had vainly been searching for in all of creation, a
creature who was "bone of his bone, flesh of his flesh", for
whom man would "leave his father and his mother". He
and she, after this, would be "two in one flesh". Here,
mutual assistance, through love and a shared life, appears
as the final cause of marriage.

Scripture, therefore, gives two essential ends of marriage,
two ends which must simultaneously be respected in order

to obey God's will, procreation and the mutual perfection or growth of the couple. These two ends must be put into some scale of values and, at the same time, their mutual implication has to be preserved.

The Primary End

The primary end must be made very clear. Pius XII clarified it in his address to Italian midwives on 29 October 1951 :

> The truth is that matrimony as a natural institution by virtue of the will of the Creator does not have as its primary, intimate end, the personal improvement of the couples concerned but the procreation and education of new life. The other ends, though also connected with nature, are not in the same rank as the first, still less are they superior to it. They are subordinated to it. This holds true for every marriage even if it bear no fruit, just as it can be said that every eye is made for seeing although in certain abnormal cases, because of special inward and external conditions, it will never be able to see.[1]

Procreation

Marriage's first end, which has indeed been made clear by nature in the complementary differences between the sexes, is to obey God's command to "increase and multiply".

We shall never be able fully to appreciate the grandeur of this task. To *procreate* a child; the word itself makes it clear that it is a collaboration with God's creative activity. While man does his ordinary human work with God's ordinary help and leaves the stamp of his humanity on whatever material creation he fashions, in his procreation he penetrates with God the very mystery of divine creation.

[1] Translation published by *The Tablet*, on November 10, 17 and 24, 1951.

This child was created by God because He gave him a soul at the point of time when human love called him into being. God fashions the human work into His image and likeness. Thanks to the co-operation of man, God invites a new being to share His life.

Procreating is giving life to a being who will have his own, unique destiny, who is completely autonomous and who is the living reflection of a light come from the heart and face of God. Creation is bringing a new creature into the living mystery of the Holy Trinity.

It means penetrating the mystery of the divine paternity, the source of all human fatherhood, and offering God a child to love. It is plumbing the depths of divine sonship, because the child will be a son in the Son, a co-heir with Christ, redeemed by the Son at the price of His blood as though he were the only person in the world. It means entering into the mystery of the Holy Spirit's sanctification, the Spirit who makes us live in holiness and whose sanctifying action will endure until the end of time. In procreation we offer Him the raw material of holiness, the clay which He will shape into an image of God's only Son.

Procreation gives the world its chief reason for existing, since "God made and tries the world only to make saints".

When we speak of a recent or impending birth in ordinary language, we call it a "happy event", as though to point out that nature itself is pleased at obeying God's law. Did not our Lord speak of the woman who forgets all her pain once she has brought her child into the world? Birth itself is a joy—and joy is an index of how far a goal has been attained. When a child is born, something eternal has been made, something sacred has been achieved. Even if a child should die on the day of his birth, he is "born in eternity", just as a priest begins to be eternally a priest at the moment of his ordination. A birth is always a success, an accomplishment. The joy it brings comes from God; not even death can rob it from the parents who have completed a divine and imperishable work.

Procreation is more than giving a child to God and the world. It seals the marriage union and brings it to complete, final perfection. It is a marriage's seal because the child is made in his mother's and father's image, as well as God's. The baby is not just a baby but, to each of the parents, he is the child the other has given, the fruit of their love. He is a living, subsistent gift that they give one another. Through this child, the "two-ness" of marriage is left behind and develops into "three-ness", as in God. Bishop Fulton Sheen has said, and rightly, that "Sexuality is duality. Love is always trinity."

Love has its own internal fecundity, even if it lacks external fecundity. In a sense, this fecundity is inherent in every marriage, even where involuntary sterility is involved. In itself, the conjugal union is procreative, though it may not, in fact, be procreating. In addition to external fecundity, there is what we might call an interior fecundity which is always present.

As Jean Guitton says:

> Love is always fertile, even when it is a matter merely of transforming the lovers. . . . Besides this external fecundity which we usually refer to, there is an internal fecundity which makes the parents themselves the first children of their love. The husband is the child of his wife; and, perhaps, the reverse may also be true, though it is less obvious. God doubtless permits sterility sometimes to distinguish internal fertility, which is essential to love, from external, accidental fertility; sterility is thus love without apparent fruitfulness. In this case, the *opus amoris* remains deep within the love; love bears, raises, instructs, helps to maturity, and gives joy to the lovers—and that is enough (*Op. cit.*, pp. 95-97).

Education

It should be noted carefully that the Church does not say that the first end of marriage is the procreation alone of children, but their procreation and education. The situation is, therefore, one which involves inseparably physical generation and spiritual generation. Parents get the primordial right to educate their children in body and soul from this unity.[1]

What every couple should do is determine the exact sense, in God's eyes, of their own conjugal vocation, according to their own circumstances. By depending on reason illumined by grace, while remaining completely obedient to God's plan for them, husband and wife will have as many children as God wants them to have, insofar as it depends on them. Once prayer and their conscience have given them a glimpse of what their family's vocation is, a couple should not be deflected by sin or selfishness from achieving it. One of the first and essential things to consider when they evaluate their circumstances in life is the education and training to give their children.

The *Family Code* of the Union of Malines, an authoritative document, discusses the size of a family thus:

> Properly understood, the law of community demands of every family community the greatest number of children which—all things being considered—the couple can not only fittingly have, but educate in a fitting manner.
>
> Every home must have its special norm for regulating the creative end of marriage.
>
> If, however, some indication must be made of the social minimum of procreativity, it could be said that an average of less than three children per home would mean the death of society by suffocation.
>
> Once this has been stated, however, it would be wrong

[1] This point is discussed in detail in our *La Question scolaire* (Bruges, 1956) and we shall not go into it here.

to believe that the law of fertility regardless of circumstances demands the greatest possible number of children.
Husband and wife must consider their personal welfare in
the matter of physical and psychological health and
strength; the welfare of their children, as regards the
best education possible for them; the family's welfare,
so far as concerns the laws of unity and order in love, and
the immediate and future welfare of the community
at large, whether national, regional or world-wide.

Parents should not forget that Providence does not fail
where it is met with generosity combined with Christian
prudence (No. 57).

Other Ends

When she speaks of the primary end of marriage, the
Church does not mean to relegate the other ends to a
secondary position, in the modern sense of the word. Nowadays, "secondary" means less important. That is not at all
what the Church means. We have to remember that when
the Church calls procreation and its necessary corollary,
education, the primary end, she means that this is the most
specific of the ends of the conjugal community which unites
two people of different sexes. All the other ends pay regard
to this orientation which is objective and inherent in all
genital activity. Here, then, is the starting-point for qualify-
ing other ends as secondary or subordinate precisely as they
are in relation to this point.

"Primary end", therefore, means the most specific end,
but all other specific ends unite with it to form a totality
whose members are interdependent and cohesive.

Therefore, this does not at all mean that the other ends as
well are not of first-rank importance. Nor does it mean that
the primary end is necessarily the uppermost on the psychological plane. So far as this is concerned, the immediate
end, felt as first, will be the mutual perfection and comple-
mentation of the couple. The most social end—the propaga-

tion of the race—will then become a more remote goal which will result from this personal communion.

The Church by no means disregards the fact that marriage is also instituted for the mutual help of the couple, when she declares that procreation and education of children is the first end of marriage. *Casti Connubii* says this explicitly:

> It is in this mutual, interior adaptation of the married couple and this careful striving to work for their mutual and reciprocal perfection, that we can really discover, as the *Roman Catechism* teaches, the cause and first reason of marriage—if we do not consider it strictly as an institution destined for the procreation and education of children, but if, in a larger sense, we see it as a common sharing of life, an habitual intimacy, a society.

Balancing the ends of marriage is rather delicate. If we put too much emphasis on the first, for example, we shall not understand why the Church allows older people, for whom procreation is no longer possible, to marry. Too much insistence on the second, as by the German Professor Doms, brings us into opposition with tradition and society's most basic needs.

Fertility and interpersonal communion, the social and personal ends of marriage, are tightly linked. As we have said, there is no reason why, psychologically, the social end, in one's intention, must take the lead from the personal end. It is enough that it is naturally inherent in the institution of marriage. Of itself, marriage implies fecundity, even if the husband and wife have no other idea than to give themselves to one another. The one purpose calls to the other, and married love ends in parenthood.

A philosopher has written that "fecundity is not an appeal from without, an external demand towards which the couple have certain obligations and rights (a *right* to a certain pleasure when they fulfil a certain *obligation*). It is the very inward appeal of their interpersonal communion when it is threatened with annihilation." Saint-Exupéry said, "Love is not looking at one another, but both looking in the same direction". A child is this "same direction", a glance in which each finds himself in going out of himself.

In this perspective and against this background we can now consider the problem of self-control and birth control.

Chapter VIII

SELF-CONTROL AND THE REGULATION OF BIRTHS

The Church's Position

WE have already said that science made a great step forward in discovering the precise periods of fertility and sterility. It was no longer impossible, as it had been, for humans to control and regulate births. Man was given the chance to co-operate willingly and deliberately with the work of procreation. He now had the key to the laws of nature in his hands, and he could use it well or ill. In itself, the key could help towards assuring, spacing or completely avoiding the birth of children. A new problem faced the moralist: to what extent may human reason influence the procreative process? May man use the non-generative periods as he likes?

The answer to this question is as complex as the reality behind it. With Pius XII, we have underlined the law of fecundity which is, of itself, inherent in every marriage contract. We must not forget what was said in the preceding chapter. The question of regulating the birth of children should not come up in a Christian conscience except in an atmosphere of generosity and confident resignation to life and God. Any solution inspired by selfishness or a fear of life is not even dreamed of here. The moral attitude to be assumed in this sphere must be drawn from the context of a totally integrated and orientated Christian life.

Pius XII spoke as clearly as could be desired about the moral lawfulness of the regulation of births. In his discourse

7

to Italian midwives, quoted above, he considered the case of a couple who would perform the marriage act during the sterile periods only :

> Nevertheless, the moral licitness of such conduct on the part of the couple would have to be approved or denied according as to whether or not the intention of observing those periods constantly was based on sufficient and secure moral grounds. . . . The marriage contract which confers upon the husband and wife the right to satisfy the inclinations of nature sets them up in a certain state of life, the married state. But upon couples who perform the act peculiar to their state, nature and the creator impose the function of helping the conservation of the human race. The characteristic activity which gives their state its value is the bonum prolis. The individual society, the people and the State, the Church itself, depend for their existence in the orders established by God on fruitful marriage. Therefore to embrace the married state, continuously to make use of the faculty proper to it and lawful in it alone and, on the other hand, to withdraw always and deliberately with no serious reason from its primary obligation, would be a sin against the very meaning of conjugal right.[1]

It is clear then that he envisaged serious reasons for permitting the exclusive use of the sterile periods in certain cases. He cites these motives in this passage:

> A couple could be excused for avoiding this positively obligatory duty [procreation] even for a long time or for the whole time of the marriage, for serious reasons such as those which are not rarely found in medical, eugenic, economic or social 'indications'. From this, then, it follows that the use of the sterile periods may not only be lawful but, in the circumstances cited, actually is.

Shortly after this talk, he expatiated upon these ideas in

[1] *The Tablet*, loc. cit.

an address to the Family Associations on 26 November 1951. After pointing out that marriage's first duty is to be at the service of life, and urging courageous generosity, he continued:

> On the other hand, the Church can sympathize with and understand the very real difficulties connected with married life in our times. Furthermore, in Our last allocution on conjugal morality, We affirmed the legitimacy, as well as the limits—which are actually quite broad—of 'regulating' births which, contrary to what is called 'birth control', is compatible with God's law. We may even hope that medical science, to which, of course, the Church leaves appraisal on the matter, will eventually be able to give sufficiently sure basis for this legitimate method. The most recent information seems to justify this hope.

We see, then, that there can be no further discussion about the lawfulness of regulating births so long as the indicated conditions really exist.

Taken separately or together, these conditions bring up some problems for a Christian couple which they must consider together in conscience, evaluating the factors present with Christian generosity. In this case, more than in others, it is the fundamental intention, the ultimate arbiter of choice, which will give their final decision its moral validity.

Limiting or Regulating

We should notice that Pius XII does not speak of *limiting* birth, birth control, but of *regulating* birth. The point is not to fix a limit to the number of children, but to space their births out over a longer period of time, putting some reasoned organization into what used to be left entirely to the procreative instinct. It is understood here that the use of man's reason in this area will be worthy of him and proportioned to the laws of life and love.

As far as birth alone is concerned, this regulation does not
envisage a smaller number of children, since a better use of
time can, on the contrary, help a mother get used to the
duties of motherhood in a more balanced way and aid her
in taking on the responsibilities with a greater reserve of
generosity and, at the same time, more physical strength.
Furthermore, it would be unjust to despise periodic continence when it is dictated by conscience.

Finally, it should be remarked that regulating births can
bring up difficulties not only for couples who have few or
no children. Some Christian homes will have to face it after
one or two children, others after seven, eight or more. It is
not a problem to small families only but for large families as
well.

Control or Instinct

Two attitudes can be held with regard to the procreative
act: we can let ourselves go along blindly with the selfishness of instinct, which demands satisfaction and will have
nothing to do with reason and, consequently, any power
that self-control may have over matter; or, on the other
hand, we can choose reasoned, voluntary procreation, considered and brought to effect in God's sight.

The first attitude is not worthy of man because it gives
free rein to instinct alone. Everyone would justifiably condemn the alcoholic who brings unfortunate children into
the world without any thought for them or his wife. There
is such a contrast between the sanctity of the procreative
act and these conditions that we would say the man had
profaned that act.

The only attitude worthy of a man and a Christian is
the one that depends upon reason and faith in performing
the act which is a supreme collaboration with God.

Human prudence, the virtue which is the usual way in
which the will of Providence is expressed, should direct and

lead instinct instead of letting it go on its own blind way. Conjugal love should be ordered; that is, it should be deliberate and the fruit of reflection and decision. Man's dignity demands that he co-operate with God's creative act with full deliberation. God gets no honour from an unthinking submission to instinct, but from a complete and perfect submission to His law, His whole law.

Prudence means "doing truth" in concord with all one's obligations. It means choosing from the entirety of complex reality what is most in line with God's whole plan for us. Prudence has to be vivified from within by the gifts of wisdom and counsel and this is why Christian families will take their decisions to prayer.

It is worthy of a Christian to perform an act of such staggering natural and supernatural consequence in complete consciousness of the act's cause. Bringing a child into the world is a sacred act; it is fitting that a couple should decide upon it once they have previously considered it before God and deliberately determined to do it, leaving nothing to chance. The expected and hoped-for child will be greeted by more love to help him develop the more his home was prepared for his arrival. This reflection, surrounded as it is by prayer, dynamized by the theological virtues and inspired by filial confidence in God, will then be an act of homage to God and help the couple in their close collaboration with the Creator Himself. Reflection and prayer are the exact opposite of egoistic self-concern. They mean that we are open to God and confident in His love.

But someone may say that to have confidence in God we must blindly put ourselves in His hands. Would not this be precisely one of the great risks that Christians face in life?

Naturally there are risks inherent in living a Christian life, but charity sometimes forbids us to take certain risks. When we do a meritorious work, our merit is not measured according to how great a risk we have run, but according to the charity motivating the act. Virtue does not grow as the obstacles to be overcome decrease—if it did, the more chaste one's life the less virtuous it would be—but according to the strength of the love for God motivating one's actions.

A Confusion to be Avoided

It sometimes happens that well intentioned but badly instructed Christians will confuse with the gross onanistic fraud a periodic continence based on natural alternation.

Onanism—its poorly chosen name matters little—is something altogether different. It consists essentially in seeking genital pleasure, a natural concomitant of the procreative act, while dissociating that pleasure from the act's natural effect and conclusion by somehow making that consequence impossible, either before, during or after the act. The serious and mortal evil of this practice lies in the fact that a person, voluntarily and by means he has chosen, has thwarted the natural end of the act he performs and which he corrupts.

Periodic continence, contrariwise, respects the natural order of things because nature itself has arranged that there be alternating periods of fertility and sterility. Pius XI said this explicitly in *Casti Connubii* : "Nor should one accuse these couples of acts contrary to nature who use their marriage right following right natural reason, even if, for natural causes due either to time [sterile periods], or certain physical defects, no new life results".

The Church has never forbidden the use of marriage in the case of sterility. We know that marriage has several ends and that the first end, procreation, may be impossible; that does not mean that the ends which pertain to the couple's mutual and common perfection cannot be attained. A similar argument may be used to legitimate periodic continence.

In all of this, we must take pains to understand precisely the Church's position. She will never say that the use of contraceptives is licit. Onanism was condemned in no uncertain terms in *Casti Connubii* which recalled all the Church's traditional teaching on the subject. What was condemned as intrinsically immoral yesterday will not become moral tomorrow. No one should entertain any confused doubt or false hope on the point; the Church has not decided these practices are immoral, she has merely confirmed what the natural law already said about them. The use of contraceptives artificially perverts an act which, by itself, would be able to tend to its reproductive end. Contraception is an essential denial of conjugal communion which it secretly disintegrates and turns into deceit and self-seeking whereas it should be an act of reciprocal giving. Over and above this, it is an attack on God's paternity, the first source of life and with which man collaborates.

This should suffice to show that periodic continence is quite a different thing from onanism.

Love and Calculation

Without condemning periodic continence on moral grounds, some people would nevertheless reject it in the name of love. They refuse to admit any influx of reason into the essentials of married life, calling it calculation and claiming that love excludes any calculation and should be left to itself.

The answer to this is that there is calculation and calculation. There is selfish calculation, seeking pleasure only and side-stepping any risks; we reject this calculation straightway as unworthy of genuine love. But we cannot call it calculation, in the pejorative sense, when a husband and wife reflect and see they are at the mercy of economic or medical circumstances which may force them to forgo having children, though they want children. Ignoring these circumstances would be selfishness, an attack on love. God gave man faith and reason to light his way and point out his road to him. Man should use them even in love.

Let this be said clearly. Anyone who uses the argument against "calculation" to defend the liberty and spontaneity of the sexual instinct is forgetting that instinct is subordinated to reason. Where would we be if we had to allow free rein, because of their natural character, to the instincts of aggressiveness, or of fear, of hunger, to preservation of self or property? A soldier who deserts his post because he is unwilling to suppress his instinct of fear and self-preservation is a traitor, and the instinct of hunger does not excuse gluttony any more than the sexual instinct does lust.

Of course, the terminal act of physical love is badly accommodated to calculation, but, again, why restrict love to its carnal aspect? True love has other dimensions. Love means more than desiring the final act of union; it also means wanting the partner's real welfare: health, sufficient wealth, living accommodation—all this has to be taken into account if an act of love is to respect a situation's total reality. Indeed, love should motivate and direct the effort to self-control, and perseverance in this effort will be a manifestation of loyalty.

By insisting that love excludes all calculation we show that true love has other ways of expressing itself than the marriage act. We have already said that periodic continence does not mean living as brother and sister, to use a current but inaccurate expression. It allows a couple the full range of physical intimacy, as we have pointed out, so long as they do not reach the terminal reflex whose absence will naturally mean that these intimacies will play a greater role than ordinarily. The "all or nothing" attitude has nothing to do with this question and we falsify the human and Christian solution by putting a couple in the position where they are faced with this dilemma: either completely terminated intercourse or nothing.

Periodic continence is something both husband and wife must practise as a couple. Even in the act of renunciation their union is deliberate and accepted by both. The expression of their love will depend on how successful they have been in developing self-control.

In themselves, a couple's acts of physical intimacy are good, desirable and necessary. Ordinarily, they perfect their union to the extent that they are not a quest for erotic pleasure, ultimately a search for self, but as much as they are the mutual self-giving which is authentic love. Here we have an indication of how much self-control is an essential part of real union.

When periodic continence becomes necessary in a home, it assumes the role and character of genuine conjugal love. The practice, which is a practical application of self-control harmonized with what nature provides, ought not to be thought of as a poor second to abstention pure and simple. In the context of a determined conjugal life, the best way to protect charity and harmony in the home should be considered the most perfect.

Part II

WHAT IS TO BE DONE?

Thus far, we have tried to sort out the chief doctrinal attitudes governing the relationship between love and self-control.

But a question immediately arises: what can be done to help people put these principles into action in their lives? The answers will vary according to the role, direct or indirect, played by those who have any responsibility in this field. We must, therefore, consider in turn each of the various social categories whose help is indispensable.

This second, practical, section will aim at clearly outlining the job of priests, doctors, researchists, parents, teachers and directors of Christian lay groups.

Their concerted and co-ordinated activity alone can answer the urgency and scope of this vital problem.

Chapter IX

THE ROLE OF THE PRIEST

An Appeal

IN a recent talk on "Holiness through Marriage" which he gave in Rome, Father Carré, O.P., made this stirring appeal to priests:

Priests today have many demands made upon them, but the problems of work or technique are not the only ones which should claim their attention.

There is, for one thing, the great and delicate gift of self which two people make to one another. Every day there are more homes looking for counsel. Grace and life bring up problems of conscience for them upon which their holiness depends as much as their apostolate.

Whether they involve the spiritual or physical relations between a couple, their love constantly exercised by purifications and expanding charity, or even the secret dialogue each one carries on with God, there are difficulties, sometimes conflicts, sometimes, even, heartbreaking conflicts.

Families are asking questions. They are looking to those men whose mission it is in the Church, under the supervision of the hierarchy, to give them light. Dare we hide this light beneath a bushel?[1]

There should be no hesitation as to what the reply to this appeal must be. It is the office of a priest to form consciences and interpret to the faithful God's thought and will, in this area more than in any other, perhaps, since it

[1] Cp. *L'Anneau d'Or* (May-August 1959), 214.

involves a moral and religious problem for so many souls.

The priest must be present as a shepherd, and we can all see how the need for his presence is, at one and the same time, essential but delicate, never-failing but discreet. He cannot disregard this appeal because, as a priest, he was instructed and prepared for it. A priest is a mediator between heaven and earth only because he has commerce in both spheres, with God and with men. And it is men who are begging him for the bread of life. The priest has to face the crucial problem on various grounds : as confessor, shepherd of souls, liturgist, preacher, moralist and organizer of the laity. We shall examine what he can be expected to do or not to do from each of these different aspects.

The Confessor

A priest in the confessional very often has to judge a case of conscience in sexual matters. The faithful frequently complain that they get differing advice on sex in the confessional and this lack of agreement disturbs them.

There is a difference between a principle and its application to a concrete case. Moral diagnoses, of course, can differ from one confessor to another, just as medical diagnoses may vary among doctors. There is a margin of relativity in the concrete application of moral principles, but the fact remains that classic cases of conscience should everywhere be handled in the same way, on the basis of a common doctrine. On this point, it might be good if priests attending local and regional "theological conferences" held in a deanery or diocese were all to make a point of regularly discussing the replies and advice they have given and then evolve a solution which would fit and be valid in most instances. Furthermore, I think that it would be well if more or all dioceses adopted the practice of one German diocese, where an official diocesan group has provided confessors with a pamphlet discussing the classic cases of marital morality and the solutions to be followed. The advice in this pamphlet is useful within that diocese—why should it not be useful elsewhere?—for the people's peace of conscience and greater instruction. More than anything else, perhaps, it is a great help in putting an end to that truly scandalous condition which so many people complain of, and which can only get worse if, failing a methodic co-ordination from us priests, things go on as they are.

All this considered, however, the laity should understand the inherent difficulty under which confession of sexual offences labours. For example, take the case of a penitent who puts his sins against chastity before a priest for judgment and sacramental pardon. Usually, he presents them strictly materially, that is, isolated from the circumstances in which they happened. Besides this, the chances are that the words he uses in his confession are vague and inadequate. More than anything else, a man like this wants, consciously or not, to be "reassured" and will be tempted to interpret the response he gets more or less as he wants to understand it. Another man may be expecting a "ready-made" answer which will enable him to put aside his own responsibility in the matter. These are exceptional cases, of course, but they are no less common for all that. A priest has to take cases like these into consideration and weigh his words very carefully.

Furthermore, the priest has to be very discreet when it comes to discussing personal details with women penitents. He is no less a man simply because he has been ordained; his priesthood is no immunity to the effects of Original Sin and women have a very precise, unchanging feminine psychology. Any dialogue between priest and female penitent, therefore, is limited. It will be immediately clear, consequently, that, so far as women and their problems are concerned, women religious, trained for the work, and women directors of women's Catholic Action or social movements can play an important part in this matter. But we shall return to this point later.

To return to our consideration of the confessor, we can see that his position can be made even more difficult if these problematic confessions most often happen around Easter or just before important feasts. Time is short then, just at the moment when the priest should be most available to be all things to all men and get right to the heart of things.

All these problems, and they are not by any means the only ones, make up the ordinary burden of suffering every priest must bear. Every priest knows what people mean when they talk about the heroism and holiness of the Curé d'Ars' long hours in the confessional. In the confessional, perhaps more than elsewhere, he realizes his role as mediator between God's light and the darkness men live in. He knows the great gap between God's holiness and man's wretchedness and he has to bridge that gap.

A priest has to be a careful guardian of God's law. He must not let it be weakened by confusion or false interpretation nor, far less, may he sanction that moral defeatism which can creep into the already threatened sphere of sexual and conjugal morality. He is the one who has to protect the indestructible marriage bond and love's sacred meaning against the whirlpools of passion. He should be absolutely unyielding to human weakness. On the other hand, he has the supreme obligation to understand it, to lead souls along the hazardous road to complete control, to point out the stages along the way and support the faithful efforts of anyone who falls but begins again with God's grace. He has to be judge and father—or, rather, he should judge as a father, with the heart of our Lord.

As a confessor, he does the inestimable service of pardoning men's sins, in Christ's name, and giving them whatever necessary counsel they need. He cannot, however, as a confessor, handle all the many aspects of the problem nor can he take upon himself the essential job of giving adequate sex instruction. Every confessor should be fully aware of the limits of his role.

If a priest is also a spiritual director, he has to develop a sense of independence in his subjects, giving them whatever advice they need but teaching them that they must get on without him. Spiritual direction is not spiritual coddling nor may a director be like a doting parent to his subjects. Direction is a liberating project and should help the subject gradually to assume his own responsibilities. The priest's attitude towards the people he is directing can be summed up neatly in St John the Baptist's dictum, "He must increase; I must decrease". This important aspect of direction can never be too much emphasized.

Perhaps we can end these considerations with a practical suggestion. Perhaps confessors could make available to their penitents small leaflets, each one discussing one of the classic moral situations. This would help solve the difficulty raised by the need for explanation and a lack of sufficient time for such explanation. The leaflets would have to be simple but to the point, lively and striking, so that the penitent either gets the information he needs or has his way paved to whatever further instruction he needs. We hope that diocesan commissions for family affairs will promote this idea and get the co-operation of moralists, doctors, psychologists and, of course, writers who are clever at putting across a message.

*   *   *

The Shepherd

A priest not only hears confessions, he is frequently also a shepherd of souls. His pastoral ministry gives him many other opportunities, at home or in church, to meet engaged couples than when they come to see him just before their marriage.

Have we a clear idea of the complexity of the pastoral problem he faces? Frequently, the engaged people he meets have never met him before, are badly instructed in their faith and, even, have not been practising Catholics since they were children. They come merely to fulfil certain legal formalities, not for genuine instruction or to get a better idea of the Church's teaching on the indissolubility of marriage, birth control, divorce, etc. So far as they are concerned, the meeting is only to clear the way for something that is really no more important in itself than the civil ceremony (where it is necessary); both are small annoyances that must be put up with. But how important it is that their ideas be changed and that they realize that marriage is a step into a sacred area, the world of the Sacraments, and that it involves not only their two lives but their personal future and the future of generations to come. Do they realize this, or have they even any idea of it?

A priest needs all the tact and diplomacy he can muster at such interviews to give them some counsel and help them see the meaning of the great Sacrament they are about to receive which will bind them to each other for life. We can understand priests' anxiety when they sometimes wonder if it would not be better simply to refuse religious marriage to some couples when it is obvious that they see no real meaning in it and, after the first difficulty, will be looking for a divorce. Some large urban areas have one divorce for every four marriages !

Let us ponder over this statistical figure. Can we be sure that people approaching marriage, which, the Church teaches, is indissoluble, understand its natural and supernatural implications? In a short time, perhaps, they will be infected with the idea of "free love" and adultery. They will have to withstand the tempting onslaughts of society's libertarianism, facilities for travelling which hinder supervision, suggestive dress, indecent performances or street advertisements and improper stage plays. What defence do we offer against this barrage of evil? Even more, where is the preventive, positive and sustained training which should make them impervious to these temptations? A priest feels all too keenly the real disproportion between the forces of good and the forces of evil facing such couples. A "last minute" meeting with future husbands and wives is one more sorrow for his shepherd's heart.

A situation like this impels us to examine our conscience. We have already seen the great gap to be filled so far as pre-marital instruction is concerned. Every possible effort should be made to correct this deficiency as quickly and effectively as possible.

For the time being, and to meet the immediate pressing need, priests should be able to give some sort of booklet or leaflet to the couples who come to them, as a supplement to the dialogue (or monologue!). It will give them a broad but comprehensive outline of the principal problems they may expect to face in marriage. There are several existing works of this type and it only needs a little thought and hard work to use them as the basis for official and obligatory booklets adapted to various intellectual levels.

Unfortunately, a project like this costs money. We do not hesitate to spend vast sums to build the churches we need, but turn stingy when it comes to putting the finishing touch to our apostolate. It is as though we had vast spiritual powerhouses but hesitated to throw the switch to carry the current by means of the booklets, pamphlets, leaflets and brochures which will give our message its concrete adaptation and take it where it is most needed.

The booklet cannot, however, be more than an interim measure. Its effect will be priceless, especially if it is well done and stimulates attention, but it will by no means make up for the deplorable deficiency we have been discussing.

As we have said, there is a shocking contrast between the

care we take to prepare candidates for the priesthood and our almost complete disregard for people about to be married, a class which includes the vast majority of the baptized faithful. No one says, of course, that it is entirely our fault; for many people, religious practices cease after Confirmation, and they have no real contact with the Church again until just before they marry.

How can any priest do what he should, in these conditions, if he must fight this battle alone and is not able to count on the organized help of the laity and parochial lay-assistants? Before moving on to the question of the indispensable co-operation of the laity, however, let us consider further the priest's role and see if the Sacrament of Marriage is fully appreciated.

*   *   *

The Priest and the Nuptial Liturgy

A liturgical viewpoint can also help us to appreciate the value of marriage. Nothing can match the liturgy's effectiveness in teaching and transmitting grace. It goes out to every man and, as it were, leads him by the hand through ceremonies and symbols to the heart of religious mystery.

The marriage ritual, as liturgy, is, therefore, very valuable. It too often still happens that the ritual is reduced to its simplest expression. In certain countries, the liturgical revival has brought on an adjustment of this situation which can only be applauded. Happily, the Belgian hierarchy, for instance, has adopted a new ritual, much of which is performed in the vernacular. According to it, the priest and his ministers meet the couple at the entrance to the church; it also includes the congregation in what is to happen, underlines the role of the couple as ministers of the Sacrament and introduces the blessing of two rings which the couple exchange as a sign of fidelity "in the name of the Father, and of the Son, and of the Holy Ghost". Those who saw the televising of the marriage of a member of Belgium's royal family were impressed by this liturgical emphasis.

This liturgical advance is a reason for rejoicing but, in our opinion at least, it would be a mistake to leave things at that. We are still a long way from bringing into bold relief the commitment the couple make of themselves to one another. The laity will appreciate any forward step on this point.

We must take into account the fact that the young couple take the most important step of their lives at the foot of the altar. For them, it is the same as a priest's ordination. It is an end to the past and a new life's beginning. The slightest word or gesture makes them alert, attentive, keen. The words and actions of the ritual are filled with significance. The priest acts in God's name and it is his mission, at this moment, to explain to the couple the meaning of their life and destiny, and to translate his words into symbolic actions.

The "I will" of the couple is so significant that it should be expanded and fully explained. This would be a worthy task for some commission of pastoral liturgy which could present its work for the hierarchy's approval.

For instance, there are the promises exchanged in the English ritual :

> I, N., take thee, N., to my wedded wife,
> to have and to hold from this day forward,
> for better for worse,
> for richer for poorer,
> in sickness and in health,
> to love and to cherish,
> till death do us part,
> according to God's holy ordinance;
> and thereto I plight thee my troth.

Even a thing like the Communist promise, used in civil marriages in East Germany, can be used as an example. Though it is heavy, clumsy and weak in meaning, it is worth quoting to show that Communist leaders, although they have no religious sense, know how to influence men at an important moment of their lives, and instinctively take advantage of the occasion to highlight the value of stability, in the state's interest:

> To all workers: We swear to make our marriage, entered into here today, a community for life. We swear to unite our active strength to bring about greater socialist conquest and more powerful workers and farmers. We swear to respect one another; to give one another every solicitude, aid and sacrifice which may be necessary; to help one another in the interest of our professional and cultural development; to conform to this ideal in all our decisions and to be unfailingly faithful to one another.

Fas est ab hoste doceri.

Once the nuptial liturgy has been fully expanded, why could there not be an annual solemn renewal of the promises, something like the Church provides for her priests during their annual retreats? We could never exaggerate marriage's sacred character and the life-giving riches it contains. This renewal would be a positive and practical way of combating the scourge of divorce and putting marital stability and the meaning of the Sacrament into sharper focus. Furthermore, it could provide an occasion for effective contact to our Catholic Action leaders and those engaged in the family apostolate.

*   *   *

The Preacher

The priest's mission includes teaching God's law, the

whole law. He has to help the faithful to know the Church's teaching on marriage, as well as its social teaching in general, of which it is a part. But how?

When a priest goes up into the pulpit on Sunday his congregation includes children as well as adults. How can he discuss these problems then?

The fact is that the people who attend Sunday Mass and whom the priest can reach only then, since they do not make retreats or days of recollection, make up the bulk of the Christian public who need instruction, direction and encouragement.

Must one wait for the parish mission, every five or six years, when the preacher can give special talks to the adults of the parish? And, in the meanwhile, do all the adults who need help have to be left in ignorance, not of the evil they know all too well, but of the means to fight against this evil?

No one suggests that every priest is any more a specialist in these problems than every doctor is, but he should have at his fingertips sufficient instruction from professional moralists which religious authority has approved.

Moreover, there is nothing to keep priests who are more specialized in these fields from offering their services to parishes other than their own for these instructions. It will mean, of course, a certain amount of reorganization of sermons for adult congregations only. But whoever desires a goal must desire the means to that goal. We have to reach the adults who do not attend conferences outside the church, so we must rely on reaching them within the church by sermons. Without the equipment to fight a strong Christian battle, these unfortunate people have a special right to our pastoral preaching.

Some strong, initial efforts such as an annual, week-long conference on family life in the parish with sufficient and complete conferences make a good start. For these

conferences, however, to be as effective as possible, the organizers would have to be sure to enlist the help of other
priests and laymen—doctors, teachers, even members of
good Christian families—to ensure a genuine interchange
of ideas and provide some sort of continuity.

*   *   *

The Moralist

If every priest has a mission to instruct the faithful on
these matters, it is the particular task of professors of ethics
and moral theology to rethink the problems raised by sex
education proportioned to the real difficulties met in
modern life. The natural law does not change, but the
application of a principle to living, concrete reality that is
clearly recognized, means that there must be a certain
amount of revision, not of doctrine of course, but of doctrine's application to actual life.

A Revision of Treatises

There is one very important job reserved for professional
moralists—rethinking and revising the classical treatises *De
Sexto*. There is new work being done, but its effect has not
been felt everywhere, especially in the lower levels of the
Christian world. The popular adaptation is not complete
yet.

Some of the treatises begin with a predetermined list of
actions considered materially, disregarding the possibility of
their being gestures of love and their basic intent. They are
primarily considered under the heading "Sin and Temptation", because this is the way a moralist or confessor has to
deal with them. A beginning like this is already doomed to
failure. We do not write about modesty in dress in terms of
inches and half-inches, but by putting the problem into
some sort of context determined by climate, custom and the

varying circumstances of time and place. The same thing applies to these moral treatises; no one should draw up a list of sins or a table of actions completely divorced from their psychological sources and bases.

What makes some of these treatises troublesome, moreover, is that they seem to imply that, more than anything else, the obligatory level of moral behaviour consists in avoiding mortal sin. This is like saying that sin in general, even venial sin, need not be a thing alien to a truly Christian conscience, as though the chief difficulty were not in helping confused consciences with God's grace and plentiful love.

Some of these treatises are ruined by their negative approach. Canon Eugène Masure, in his *Recherches de la famille,* says this:

> The presentation of sexual morality in our catechisms and manuals ... seems frankly negative: the whole discussion is of bad thoughts, bad looks, bad actions. There is barely room for suspecting even that there are such things as good thoughts, good looks, good actions.
>
> Even less do they allow us to realize that evil is not necessarily in thoughts, looks or actions themselves, but in the man who thinks, looks or performs an action following an impulse of intent or the will which is not good.
>
> Briefly, the same material act, using *material* in Aristotle's sense, changes completely according to its intellectual or spiritual form which combines with the indeterminate, material, element to make a complete whole which alone can be morally judged (p. 269).

Listening to the Laity

Moralists cannot do this work successfully unless they also enlist the aid of the laity. Doctors, psychologists, psychiatrists and even married people can be priceless sources of information.

A moralist has to apply stable principles to a reality which changes as it becomes better known. An exchange of ideas in dialogue can only be worth while, not to bring up new principles, but to collate principles with real situations. The stakes—grace in souls—are too high not to distinguish very carefully between good and evil, and not to take advantage of every opportunity to set up a solid and universal doctrinal line.

Even today we hear of disagreement among moralists and the list of their variations down through the centuries is, unfortunately, all too long. Close contact with well informed and conscientious laymen could be a touchstone for judging whether one or another solution is actually morally and psychologically liveable. Moralists would also benefit by more closely examining human acts, in the context of life's dynamism, because we run the risk of misconstruing an act's deepest motivation when we extract it from the context of life.

As Father Plé, in an article in *Vie Spirituelle* (No. 36, 1956), wrote :

> Most treatises on Christian morality and catechisms restrict their material to an investigation of the moral conscience of the Decalogue. That is why they lose sight of the dynamism of the subject. They are the expression of a very legitimate juridic mentality, but one which is incomplete and needs to be re-focused by genuine theology, which is the study and wisdom of God.
>
> In the light of this 'theological spirit', morality is essentially the study of man's road to God. It studies the dynamism and the actions through which man finds perfection and happiness on that road to God (p. 6).

Moralists have a magnificent and irreplaceable role to play. We can make this clearer, perhaps, by an analogy. When Bernadette said that "the Lady wants a chapel built and she wants people to come in procession", her words set in motion a chain-reaction of co-operation. People collected materials, laid out roads, constructed hotels and built bridges. All this because of a few words spoken by a child.

Something like this happens when moralists tell us about the laws of conjugal morality. We expect them to explain the law to us, but they have also to lay out the roads we have to follow in obeying the law and to give directions *en route* for obeying it in complete fidelity to God. They have the serious and noble duty to make the road to the sanctuary clear and straight, and to build bridges between human weakness and God's law which is, at bottom, the law of human happiness.

The Priest Encouraging the Laity

A priest's duties do not end with teaching morality and preaching. He also has to talk to others and stimulate them to activity. It is terribly important to put truth within men's reach. Giving them ideas about truth in general and universal truths is not enough; they have to be directed into applying general principles to themselves and putting them into action.

A priest, too, has to talk with men in their homes and teach them, in conversation, what life and love mean. Occasions like this are excellent opportunities for dealing with various pastoral problems. He can give the necessary individual instruction that is otherwise difficult when the natural intimacy of a home makes confidences easier and stimulates an exchange of points of view, so that husband and wife can bring up together the problems they have and work out their radical solution. Teaching right in the home is one of the chief duties of pastoral activity which is genuinely adapted to life.

Everyone, however, realizes how complicated and delicate

the presence of a priest in a home can be. Gabriel Marcel's highly successful play *Croissez et multipliez-vous* brought out the problem with great impact. Though the priest in the play was badly equipped for his job, the point of the story was no less real just because the play may, therefore, have been a little forced. The problem becomes doubly difficult because of a lack of proportion and of time: how can a priest hope to have enough time to reach all the homes in his care? How many of these visits can a priest in a city parish make?

Family groups are growing and each of them would like the services of a priest; this fact underlines still more boldly the need we face of rethinking the apostolate to families along the lines we envisage. A priest cannot allow himself to be monopolized by a few families, but must be at the beck and call of all of them when they ask for his help. There is only one way out for him—he has to form some *élite* families into pilot-families. He has to help them develop a sense of Christian influence and give them the spark they must pass on to their neighbours. Once more we come back to the question of co-operation with the laity and lay parochial assistants.

The work to be done is tremendous and has many, many facets. All initiative must be co-ordinated but, first of all, whatever is done has to be thought out along the lines laid down by the problems at hand.

From all of this distress, at least one important beginning has been made. The Belgian bishops recently decided to form a National Centre for Family Pastoral Activities. It has been founded with a threefold objective in view.

The first goal of the Centre is doctrinal, considered theoretically as well as methodologically. In the light of present circumstances, it was decided that an essential task is encouraging research and study to the end that the Church's traditional doctrine on marital and family morality may be the better understood and taught. In this way, doctrinal studies will be made real and systematically organized, instead of being spread out over a large area. The Centre will act as a consultative commission to which will be submitted beforehand any writings intended for publication in the sphere of conjugal morality or family pastoral activity. The commission will thus be analogous to the national liturgical commission.

Secondly, while not constituting a new branch or movement of Catholic family action, the Centre will be charged with supervising the doctrinal formation of counsellors and those giving conferences. These people's work will be to explain Christian teaching during many pre-marital meetings, or to help engaged couples or husbands and wives who come to marriage guidance councils. The Centre will also be engaged in studying the principles fundamental to preparation for marriage and the possible means of instructing engaged couples before they meet with their parish priest for a canonical examination.

The Centre's third task will be a careful co-ordination of the many family apostolate activities, such as family study groups, consulting offices, etc. Priests will play the chief role in this co-ordination and will be appointed responsible chaplains or moderators of one or another of the groups or movements. In this way, the Centre will ensure that these many efforts, which we are fortunate to have and which are so essential right now, will not fall by the wayside and cease developing, but will more and more grow into their rightful place in the apostolate in general.

These are the main avenues of activity which have already been planned and which, in our opinion, cover a great deal of the work to be done.

We sincerely hope that the Centre will effectively help priests carry out their duties to families as organizers and inspirers of lay people. This role of the priest has many facets, but one, contact between priests and the medical world, should especially be singled out. The priest will find his first collaborators among doctors and he should go first to them to ask for their help and encourage them to take on vocations to the family apostolate, which we shall consider in detail later.

There has to be a co-operative effort between priests and doctors. We do not dissociate the soul from the body ordinarily, and in this field, especially, such a dissociation would be unreasonable. We are wrong if we say that the spiritual aspect of the problem is the priest's business, and the physical aspect the doctor's. This would be dualism and completely unrealistic. Priests and doctors have to take care of the integral human entity, under different, but complementary, aspects. In this partnership, the priest is the organizer and guide on the doctrinal level, while the doctor, enlightened and instructed by the Church, brings the Church's thought to its logical and concrete conclusion and application. Together they are, in some way, the Church teaching on this subject, and so they appear to the faithful. Their vocabularies may differ, but they reason in the same way and the conclusions of their activities are identical.

This would seem the time to discuss the doctor's vocation in the apostolate of the family.

CHAPTER X

THE ROLE OF THE DOCTOR

THERE is a strong link between the priest's role and the doctor's. They have to co-operate in training men to self-control and, without their firm, complementary and combined efforts, the struggle will go on without its first condition for success. Each of them has to give and receive in turn, according to their roles. The priest takes care of doctrine and its moral implications, while the doctor's part involves knowing the ways and means available to a common idea of man's nature and destiny.

The doctor is particularly qualified to play a leading role in the task of instructing people to sexual control in marriage, a task which is, at the same time, eminently human and religious. His first task will be to become aware of his mission and to listen to St Paul, "See what your vocation is".

A Christian Doctor—or a Doctor who is also a Christian?

Which is more correct, to speak of a Christian who is a doctor, or a doctor who is a Christian? At first sight, the question seems otiose. But the fact is that it puts the problem squarely: Is a Christian doctor first a doctor and then a Christian, or is he above all a Christian who practises medicine?

We need not hesitate about giving the correct answer. A baptized person, doctor or not, is first of all a Christian. This position is fundamental, and with the Christian doctor his being baptized a Christian is his dominant and

substantial quality. Christianity is the first duty of his state
in life and all the others have to be harmonized with it. It
is the spirit underlying all his professional obligations.

The Doctor and Christ

The doctor is linked with Christ in an extraordinary
bond. Our Lord came to save men and to heal them. "I
have not come for those who are well," He said, "but for
those who are sick." Of course, He especially meant those
who were spiritually sick, but He did not forget suffering
bodies. Healing runs through His life like a strong thread,
and the Gospels are filled with Christ's healing gestures. A
woman touches the hem of His garment and is cured of
chronic haemorrhage; He mixes His saliva with soil and a
blind man sees; paralyzed people stand, take up their pallets
and walk at His touch or command; fevers break; sick
people, far away from Him, return to health at the moment
Jesus prays for them. Even the dead return to life at His
voice, and Lazarus leaves his tomb. Our Lord's compassion
is like the watermark of the paper on which the Gospels are
written, and it touches bodies as well as souls.

Christ, the chief healer of the world, did in instantaneous
and supreme gestures what medical science, subordinated
to time in the battle against disease, gropingly tries to
do. There is a very special bond indeed between Christ
and doctors, a secret link which, through other ways and
means, is something of an extension of His mission in
Palestine.

The sick man who looks up to a doctor for help sees in the
man taking care of him a glimmer of Christ's mercy. He
gives the doctor something of the confidence and humility
he has before a priest. Man is a whole and he knows that
Christ is the Saviour of that integrity. As he lies on his sick
bed, priest and doctor are in the image of God's Son and
are ministers of a single, identical compassion.

Sick people put themselves entirely into the hands of their doctor, giving him not only their injuries and wounds to heal, but their whole lives if they feel he has the slightest fatherly interest in them. A doctor becomes more than a therapist who takes care of one or another complaint; he is the good Samaritan who not only pours oil onto their wounds but also, and more important, takes complete charge of them and, if he can, gives them shelter.

The doctor's vocation dovetails with the priest's; its nobility springs from his delicate familiarity with man down to the roots of his being. Everyone knows the strong authority and confidence a doctor enjoys with sick people who open their hearts to him.

A doctor is an expert manager of men; his psychological talents are an integral part of his medical gifts. His Christian influence can work on his patients, whether they realize it or not, in the same way as the ultra-violet rays which he focuses on them to heal them. Pascal looked for the man in every writer; every sick person consciously or otherwise looks for the saving and healing Christ in every doctor.

The Doctor and Man

Better than anyone else, a doctor knows he is not taking care of a body only but of a man, an animated body, an incarnated soul. He must care for the whole human complex. If he is responsible for a man's health, he is responsible for the whole man's health; making distinctions and precisions in this matter is not human nor is it Christian. Pius XII said to a group of Italian cancer researchers that, "before everything else, a doctor has to consider the entire man in the unity of his person, that is, not only his physical condition, but also his psychology, his moral and spiritual ideals and his place in society".

Catholic doctors should lead the field in this integral

medicine which appeals to spiritual and moral factors, takes into account the slightest psychological repercussion and circumstances of a course of treatment and is keenly aware of interaction and interference between the soul and the body. He must never forget that even though a bodily injury may not affect the soul, a hurt to the soul affects the body. Sin inevitably brings on a loss of balance. Every time we break one of God's commandments it is written in our living body and somehow causes disquiet, destroying joy, which is essential even to physical health. Many, many neuroses have their roots in a denial of Christ.

The affliction we are concerned with is sexual disturbance, which has brought on many collapses and is far less exempt from this rule than any other disorder. This is one more, urgent, reason for a Christian doctor to do all he can to re-establish threatened harmony in that area.

The Doctor and Sexual Disturbance

The sick man we are concerned with in this book is the man who has lost, but must recover, his self-control. A doctor who has grasped what his Christian vocation is will see in that situation an appeal for his co-operation in fighting for humanity as it really is.

If, according to Lacordaire's magnificent definition, a Christian "is a man to whom Jesus Christ has confided other men", then a Christian doctor is a man who, of all men, has been given other men to help, rehabilitate and save. His medical profession will be his particular way of working out this common obligation of all the Church's children.

He has been given a very special care of humanity which is thrown off balance by Original Sin. This trouble, this deep-rooted disturbance that has so many human variations, is his particular territory, his field of action, his branch of the Christian apostolate. Actually, the neighbour put in his care is all suffering humanity. A doctor should never forget the breadth and depth of his obligation.

A doctor is expected to try to restore man to what was God's original idea for him. In the beginning, man, created in God's image, was organized and balanced. Body submitted to soul and the soul was submissive to God. That was man's condition at the dawn of creation before Original Sin disrupted this majestic harmony. The doctor meets the effects of Original Sin every day, and it is his task to do what he can to restore in man his resemblance to God, initial rectitude and, generally, God's original plan.

It is a majestic task in any area, but most especially in the sexual sphere where man's control of himself is a work of re-organization affecting his entire destiny. It means working with the Holy Spirit to whom this healing is especially appropriated by the Pentecost hymn:

> *Lava quod est sordidum,*
> *Riga quod est aridum,*
> *Sana quod est saucium,*
> *Flecte quod est rigidum,*
> *Fove quod est frigidum,*
> *Rege quod est devium.*

> Heal our wounds, our strength renew;
> On our dryness pour thy dew;
> Wash the stains of guilt away :
> Bend the stubborn heart and will;
> Melt the frozen, warm the chill;
> Guide the steps that go astray.

By definition, every Christian is universal and should not have a narrow or limited outlook towards the world immediately around him. Every baptized person and every doctor can say, "The whole world is my parish". Consequently, a doctor will look beyond the narrow horizon of his own patients; he has a mission to save the world and add his own contribution to its salvation, nothing more or less will do. His vocation as a Christian goes beyond helping sick people, the work he does, no matter how noble, to earn his living. Like every other Christian, he has to help his fellows to bring the whole Gospel into every area of their life, and he is deeply involved in the business of handing on Christian life to the whole world. It is not the perquisite of the clergy. The wellspring of the Christian apostolate is the baptismal font, and everyone bears on his forehead the chrism of Confirmation which blessed him as an instrument of life and salvation.

Doctors have a special and irreplaceable function in making God loved and His law obeyed. They are more strictly held to their obligation than others because they see and feel the effects of obedience, peace and happiness, and the effects of disobedience, tears and collapse.

Over and above his strictly professional obligations, he has to take care of all suffering, groping and stumbling humanity and devote himself to helping it. The very immensity of the task should impel him to find adequate solutions.

The Doctor as Trainer of Co-operators

By himself, the doctor is powerless, even in countries where the ratio between the size of the population and the number of doctors is adequate. But what about the vast countries where the ratio is almost ridiculously small? Ordinary doctors who have a general practice are not the ones to give sex education, supposing that they were asked to. Nor are specialists. Will it, then, be the sexologist, who has been specially trained in this field? Christian sexologists are very rare and do not exist in many countries. But we shall consider this major deficiency later.

The problem is further complicated when we recall that

instruction in sexual control is needed not only by people who are in some way sick, but even by healthy people; in fact, the vast majority of adults need it. Shall we, consequently, give up the idea of having doctors co-operate? Not at all; doctors, however, should be ready to step in and instruct and train people who will instruct and train others. General practitioners and specialists can do that because their general medical background has equipped them for the work. All doctors, therefore, are included in the call for help. There is room for helpers from every level of humanity, provided only they have good will and are ready to do the work assigned them.

The doctor's role can be described briefly as a willingness to train co-operators.

Where do we find Collaborators?

There is no need to search very far for these collaborators. A doctor's immediate surroundings will provide them in plenty. He will find them in the whole stratified medical world he lives in: hospital nuns, nurses, midwives, social workers, laboratory technicians, pharmacists, nursing and medical students. The entire environment is a natural breeding-ground for workers in this new field of assistance. Doctors will have to convince their co-workers that they can help them, and then it will be up to them to train them and give them whatever formation they need. They will have to see that their new collaborators get the instruction they need either from others or from the doctors themselves, instruction which should go beyond the ordinary level of medical knowledge and is more orientated towards the field of sexual morality. Psychological training will help them to teach others with tact, precision and clarity. The job can be done and it is worth the effort involved. So many other professions and projects take much more time and effort and are not nearly so involved in the salvation of souls.

Once the doctor has organized the people in his professional field into helping him, he will find more helpers among teaching religious and zealous men and women belonging to various Catholic organizations and movements. Gradually, his influence and teaching will reach more and more people.

An example of the work which a doctor can do are the classes given to women religious by Dr Le Moal of the Children's Neuropsychiatric Clinic in Paris, and his lectures to teachers of young people, published as *Éducation et rééducation sexuelles* (Oeuvre national d'aide à la jeunesse, Brussels).

More work like this should be undertaken. Moralists have to supervise the doctrinal instruction of doctors, but the doctors will have to apply what they have learned and bring it down to everyone's level.

It is to be earnestly hoped that a growing number of doctors will take on this task of popularization, in the good sense of the word, and help the many nascent family groups now in various stages of formation. Every army has superior officers who give commands, and lower officers who hand on and explain those commands. A doctor is like a superior officer and should be able to organize his regiment, make his goals clear, and choose the right people to execute the commands leading to those goals.

The Woman Doctor

Women doctors have an especially large part to play in this variegated apostolate. They are better qualified than anyone else to take care of instructing women and for working out projects which take into account feminine psychology and reactions.

It would do us good to realize that many women play a

major part in modern neo-Malthusian movements. With a stubborn courage that deserves a better cause, they organize campaigns which eat into Christian morality and give materialism an even tighter grip on modern society.

But what about our women? All too few of them are ambitious enough to use their knowledge and devotion for the cause we are promoting. Is it their fault? Has this kind of work been suggested to them?

Whatever the cause may be, it would be a good thing if priests, retreat masters and teaching religious focused the attention of young women on a career which can do so much good if it is orientated in this direction.

Happily, woman's new place in society makes a medical career possible for her. It is highly desirable, however, that more women doctors would specialize in the branches of medicine most pertinent to the family, motherhood and children. They could be such a great help, because of their perception and delicacy, in bringing grace and, consequently, life in Christ to an area of life which is too often disorganized, without harmony and sinful. When a Christian chooses a career, surely his criterion should be where and how he can best extend God's kingdom among men?

The Price to be Paid

There will be many objections to this appeal to all Catholic doctors, and the greatest obstacle is a limited view of the duties of one's professional life. It is so easy to exaggerate loyalty to one's duties as a professional person to the detriment of one's duties as a Christian. Baptism places us in a state in life which has its peculiar obligations and these obligations form the background for any further obligations. Can anyone deny that every man has many duties in his life which must all be fulfilled simultaneously?

Catholic doctors have to respect the divine will which

has put their obligations into a certain hierarchical order. A doctor could be tempted to believe that the best use of his time is the one that leaves him most free to take care of the largest number of patients, but that would be incorrect reasoning. The best use of his time is the one that helps him increase his personal efforts to help his neighbour. The time spent in the training we have been discussing is pre-eminently useful and advantageous to the human community.

There is no reason for him to be mistaken about who his neighbour is. The Gospel tells him: you will find your neighbour in Jerusalem and in Judea, but in Samaria, too, and all through the world. God has given the Christian doctor his neighbours, and they are not only his own patients, but all unbalanced humanity, the victims of sexual disorder. And humanity includes many, many people who are not physically ill and whose names are not in any medical register.

The few hours that he takes away from his regular practice from time to time, to give them to another, larger and anonymous, list of people who need his help and whom he will help through trained collaborators, should be almost holy to him, since Christ Himself asks for the time. He should offer this time freely and generously, as his personal contribution, as a Christian doctor, to the work of extending God's kingdom. This renunciation, this detachment from money-making will be the offering that makes him worthy of the beatitude, *beati pauperes,* blessed are the poor. As his professional success grows, and his patients become more and the temptation to close himself up in his consulting room increases, he will have a stronger battle to wage. But he must leave the doors and windows of his soul open to the world's cries for help.

The Reward

Christ will be moved by the doctor's gesture, so like what the good Samaritan did, more than by anything else he may do because God's mercy goes first of all to whomever is most in need of it. God sees the glass of water given to the thirsty man and He will remember it on the day "when we shall be judged according to our love". A special reward has been promised to those who help men to obey God's law. A doctor who has helped others to obey God's commandments will have a special right to God's mercy, which is one with heaven's beatitude.

The few hours a doctor takes away from the narrowly defined obligations of his state in life to fulfil his broader obligations as a Christian will have an incomparably rewarding effect upon men. Surely it is clear how a doctor's activity can help the work of a priest? Both of them are building up Christianity. If the doctor points out the havoc divorce brings into homes, from his own point of view, while the priest denounces divorce on moral grounds, the effect of their co-ordinated action will be doubled. Doctors, then, should strike out against every menace to home life, one by one from alcoholism to prostitution and homosexuality, which is growing more and more widespread and outstrips all other sexual problems. Their efforts will reinforce the work of priests and both together will be an unshakeable buttress against the collapse which threatens too many of our homes. That great doctor Alexis Carrel pointed out that prayer has something of a curative and medicinal property, and his idea has had astonishing effect. We can rest assured of the good results of a doctor-priest co-operative action which treats the whole man and teaches him the same divine law while helping him to develop Christ's life within his soul.

The Doctor as a Social Agent

A doctor's work will mean not only helping his patients and helping others through the collaborators he has instructed, but being effective in society as a whole. A family is not like an island in the sea, but like a cell in a living being; whatever threatens the life of the whole being is also a threat to its cells. More than anyone else, a doctor realizes that sexual education and re-education depend to a great extent upon our environment. It is up to him, therefore, to stimulate public opinion, the world of legislators and journalists, responsible members of government and law courts, and to strike out against anything in our laws or customs which prejudices public health. He must, consequently, fight against anything which prevents or frustrates sexual education or re-education.

Doctors have to wage war on whatever weakens or poisons homes, or kills Christ's life in souls. Each doctor's responsibility for public health means he has to take up arms against prostitution, divorce, masturbation, sexual deviation, abortion and direct sterilization. Anything pertaining to the laws of health strongly affects man's deepest dynamism. Doctors have to be the watchmen over everything that helps men live as men, and Christians as Christians. He has all the modern means of communication at his disposal to achieve this purpose.

Doctors should use radio or television themselves, or encourage their use by others, for this purpose, or should make films the vehicles for propaganda. There have been films on medical themes—painless childbirth, for instance—which were basically sermons encouraging generous motherhood. Newspapers can be used as tribunals of judgment to form right opinion and excoriate unnatural vice. Social and charitable Catholic Action movements can be enlisted, and doctors can make them relay stations for transmitting their message more and more deeply into all levels of society.

Doctors know the value of communication services in fighting physical disease; think of the marvellous campaign they are fighting against cancer. But there are also moral cancers gnawing away man's most vital fibres. Doctors have to enlist all the aid they can and avert disaster by curing the moral cancers attacking family life and conjugal love. They should even be eager to give new knowledge to the teaching Church about those plagues with which they more than anyone else come into close contact, and which raise problems of conscience that moralists must study.

Social Organizations of Christian Doctors

If we are genuinely interested in achieving these social goals, then our battle has to be more than a series of skirmishes; the time has passed when individual workers or sociological dilettantes were enough. If Christian doctors want to make their influence felt, they must organize.

Of course, it is a good thing if they belong to professional groups which are neutral so far as concerns religion. By defending the natural law and its right application in these organizations, they also defend God's law. There still remains, however, the need for an organization of Christian doctors. It should extend to the national level but also be international, because today's big projects and campaigns are all waged on an international scale.

Rome has, with good reason, constantly called on Christian doctors to appreciate the real urgency there is for them to organize in an international way. Catholics have especially to be vigilant and drawn up in close battle formation against the obvious or hidden influence of neo-Malthusianism in world health organizations. They cannot expect to win the battle if each one is left to range freely over the field.

I should like to quote here the appeal I made in my speech at the opening of the first Catholic World Congress of Health:

The Congress gives you the opportunity to consider your corporate or individual role as Christians in the world today. We are not living in the world alone, but in a world which can no longer be called Christian. Our task in the world is to be the leaven the Gospel speaks of.

But how can we respond to our vocation as Christians along all its dimensions? I know that this problem worries you all, and the Church expects that you will take another, closer, look at it from the viewpoint of your lives as professional men.

Right now there are many kinds of organizations for doctors and people associated with the medical profession.

There are professional groups whose members are both Catholics and non-Catholics and whose professional interests are entirely general.

There are also organizations which can be called 'Catholic Action' groups, and their chief aim is the spiritual life of their members.

Finally, there are Catholic professional groups which are involved with both the professional and spiritual lives of their members.

It seems that there is a genuine need at the present time for Catholic professional organizations whose members and directors, however, must understand the role they play on the professional plane as well as the spiritual— and how they have to involve the group as well as individuals, and international activity as well as national.

Catholic professional groups will be incapable of fulfilling this mission until each of them is well organized.

Consequently, time has to be spent in studying a way towards a national co-ordination of organizations for Catholic doctors and other medical workers.

Co-ordination on the international level will make it possible to concentrate resources, work out a plan of study and allocate activities according to the varying needs of established or developing countries.

Co-operation like this will generate strength and stimulate interest, making the members of the various medical professions more aware of their world-wide responsibility.

This co-ordination will make it possible to collaborate with, and thereby render more influential, non-religious international organizations working in all medical and medico-social fields.

A possibility like this, let us repeat, can only be realized if contact with non-religious groups, national or international, is made on the professional level.

We earnestly hope that the future will see this suggestion realized. Catholicism's strength in social fields has been weakened by liberalism for too long. Now is the time, in this field as well, for us to assert ourselves in order to co-operate better, as Christians, in founding the earthly Kingdom.

Before closing our discussion of the connection between the work of the priest and of the doctor in sex education, it might be well to take a quick look at two more areas of this co-operation which could be very fruitful.

Doctors meet Moralists

Everything said so far naturally brings up the point that doctors and moralists should work together to exchange points of view, give one another the benefits of experience and clear up any misunderstandings arising from different technical languages.

We can consider two examples of this last point. Much confusion could spring from the different meanings of the word "contraceptive". When a doctor talks about "contraceptive practices" he means, effectually, anything which prevents a birth, all the way from complete continence to criminal abortion. A moralist, however, uses the term to designate immoral practices only. He uses the word pejoratively, while the doctor uses it technically and in a morally neutral sense. Likewise, any phenomenon which occurs frequently, such as masturbation in puberty, is "normal" to a doctor. When a moralist says "normal", however, he means spiritually healthy, licit, according to the norm of morality.

If these meetings are going to be productive, they cannot stop at the level of conferences and discussions. They should be followed up by co-operative, directed and methodical activity. They have to be springboards into decisive campaigning with clearly defined goals. Here, again, planning, imagination and courage will be needed to go right down into the mass of humanity and, sleeves rolled up, get down to solid work.

A Service to be Given

Priests are indispensable to doctors as doctrinal guides and advisors, but doctors can also be of great, complementary assistance to priests.

Help from medical men will be very useful not only during a priest's seminary days, but during his ministry, too. Lectures by doctors, followed by frank and direct conversation, are inestimably helpful during a seminarian's or novice's training. Priests need balanced, mature and clear training about sexual matters, especially, for themselves and others.

A Swiss priest, Father Jakob Crottogini, has published a psycho-pedagogical thesis on the priesthood, and one of the points of his investigation covered the connection between sexual control and vocation. The number of seminarians who complain of not having received enough instruction in the matter is striking.[1]

The ability of a competent doctor, motivated by deep faith and equipped with psychological sensitivity, is an excellent complement to a scholastic training which runs the risk of being too abstract, or spiritual direction which may not be practical enough. On the strictly practical level,

[1] *Werden und Krise des Priesterberufes* (Benziger Verlag: Einsiedeln, 1955). See also "Crise et devenir du sacerdoce", *Vie Sprituelle*, 49 (1959).

a doctor can help in character formation and self-control by offering his peculiar professional knowledge.

Doctors can give the same help to priests who often come to grips with many pastoral problems connected with family life in their ministry. It would also be a great help to have doctors explain to them the medical consequences of the social disorders against which, with doctors, they must fight.

CHAPTER XI

THE ROLE OF UNIVERSITY PEOPLE AND SCIENTISTS

A UNIVERSITY is a focal point of higher education and scientific research. Because of this double quality, the co-operation of Catholic members of universities and scholars is necessary for the indispensable work of sexual rehabilitation and training.

Let us examine what can be done in universities, by students and by teachers.

Students

Because they are *students*, university students should be in a position to receive the benefits of a positive, university-level, training which is also practical and which responds to their intellectual, moral, as well as religious, needs. By definition, a student is more than just someone who studies; he is a person whose heart and affections are awakening.

Many students become engaged to marry while still at university; their emotional and sexual needs bring up immediate problem, and in the future they will need to know what the Church expects of them so far as married love and self-control are concerned.

Considering a student as an intellect only is a bizarre kind of shortsightedness. He is on the brink of adulthood and wants an adult solution to his secret or admitted problems which are very often connected with religion. He has come to the point where he demands new reasons for belief, reasons proportioned to his adult conscience. For him, problems of faith and problems of morality have to be solved together.

There is room in universities for a series of courses on these matters, courses which could be introduced into the regular programme and which would have their own orientation, being adapted to the students of the various faculties. Law students need the same knowledge and training as future teachers and engineers; the emphasis, however, will be different while the principal ideas will be the same for all.

A doctor who is now engaged in the family apostolate wrote the following about his years at university:

> I can testify that the training for life was not given in a way proportionate to normal living. Many problems were passed over in silence. People too often forgot that young people will, eventually, have to take on serious responsibilities. Problems of human psychology, of sexual education and of life in general were not raised at the university but were taken care of by small private organizations outside the official programme, which were able to deal with a limited number of students only. Most students were thrown into university life, filled as it is with snares, without the slightest preparation or orientation. They knew nothing of psychology in general, of the psychology of sex, nor of feminine psychology.
>
> Heaven knows that knowledge like this is absolutely necessary, not only for those whose careers will put them into contact with the public (lawyers, magistrates, social workers, nurses, engineers, educational administrators, teachers, etc.), but also for those who plan to establish families.

The training that is needed, let us repeat, is not only intellectual; it has to cover every field of natural and supernatural education. This implies that the training will be individualistic in approach and that there will be the possibility of personal contact with the people who are competent to form characters and consciences in the great world of the university. Such a suggestion does not overlook the difficulties arising from the size of the university population. One practical approach would be to break the university body down into groups small enough so that the adult of tomorrow, lost in the crowd, can be reached. It is a problem deserving our best and most courageous efforts. To a great extent, the future of our young people in universities and of the families of tomorrow depends upon it.

Medical Students

In view of what we have seen as the role of the doctor, it is clear that special care must be taken with teaching future doctors. If we ask what is being done in this field, however, we must honestly answer, "Nothing". So far as I know, not a single Catholic university in the world gives a course in Christian sexology. Until this gap is filled, these questions have to be taken up in courses of medical ethics and other fields directly touching on them, such as gynecology and neurophysiology. No matter how indirectly, these important problems have to be highlighted and studied.

It is of the highest importance that future doctors be instructed to the limit in the exacting field of the medical aspects of periodic continence, not only for their own knowledge, but so that they can instruct others. They have to be able to direct others along the double road of self-control and control of the natural variations in the feminine cycle.

For their own control, they should know about all the most recent advances of science and have confidence in their effectiveness for themselves and others. Defeatism has never won a battle and, besides, it would be unscientific in a doctor.

For controlling nature, they have to know the legitimate

methods of spacing births, so that they can explain them to others in the future and help them avail themselves of these methods. Too many people find fault with the miscalculations that can be connected with the Ogino-Knaus method or the temperature curve method. Discreet enquiries would show that, in many cases, whoever explained the method did so in a careless and superficial, if not inaccurate, way. Before accusing a horse of kicking up in the ranks, we should find out if the cavalryman knows how to sit him properly. It is too easy to disdain and condemn those methods which, despite their limitations, morality allows us to use for the good of our consciences. But we shall come back to these methods below.

Just because a medical student intends to specialize in cardiac surgery or ophthalmology does not mean that he can disregard these matters. Every Catholic doctor, as such should be ready to take his place in the ranks of the rehabilitating forces.

Souls must grow or remain in the state of grace and they will need a superabundance of help and effort from Catholic university people who, like priests, are responsible for their neighbour's salvation. The man who works towards his brothers' redemption is closely involved in the mystery of life and death which lies at the heart of Christianity.

The Professors

In view of this mission, it seems urgently necessary that Catholic universities establish a course in sexology wherein all these problems would be examined in the light of Catholic teaching. We must never be suspicious or dubious about the subject of sexology, but we can question the way it is treated by some experts, especially if they are materialists. In itself, the science of human sexual behaviour deserves careful scientific study because of its repercussions

on everyday life. The point is that these problems should
be studied in the light of Christ, objectively.

The problem here is something like what happened in
the motion picture industry. The absence of Catholics from
the industry for too long a time made the screen a play-
ground for exploiters of human passion. Nowadays, we
understand things better and see that there are almost
infinite opportunities for winning souls through films. We
shall not win by boycotts or condemnations, but by being
actively engaged in the industry.

The same holds true in the science of sex. It is too often
presented wrapped up in a philosophy that denies man's
real nature. A philosophy like that, however, is not the
necessary vehicle for this science. Better than anyone else,
Catholic scholars are equipped to locate sexology in an
integrated context, human and Christian, and to study its
laws with tranquil objectivity. Looked at in this way, this
science could be a priceless aid to achieving indispensable
self-control.

Christian sexology as such has the right to be listed on
the programmes of our medical schools. It has its own formal
object : the human couple as such. It should stop being
considered a sort of *terra ignota,* as appeared on old maps,
or an imprecise field of knowledge in which several medical
sciences overlap.

Sexology is neither endocrinology nor gynecology nor
psychopathology, for all that these subjects are connected
with it. It must no longer be the territory left free to
materialists or unbelievers. It is a mission field waiting for
Christian influence in much the same way as the most distant, pagan countries are. More and more state universities
are opening courses in sexology, some of them Institutes of
Sexology, on the same footing as other branches of human
learning. While waiting for a similar opening in Catholic
universities, some of our professors would be performing

a worthwhile service by preparing a few of their better students for this specialization.

Every specialization, of course, is valuable, but this is one where the Catholic doctor, more than elsewhere, can use his special talents. Medical students, furthermore, should be told that there are some branches of medicine of special interest to the Church and in which she would like to see many of them working. An apostolic consideration like this, basic to their choice, could make their lives as Christians very full indeed. It would be a good thing if, when students have theses to write, laboratory research to do or some special work to do, Catholic medical faculties would draw their attention to work in this field. Work like this has an obvious Christian reward in addition to its scientific value.

All this brings us quite naturally to the contribution which men of science, in their turn, can make towards solving the problem we have been discussing. Though their role may be hidden and indirect, it is no less essential, since it involves the future of medicine.

Scientists

We come, then, to research scientists and what the Church expects of them.

Speaking at the first Catholic World Congress of Health at the Brussels Exposition in 1958, I gave the following outline of a response:

Permit me to appeal for your co-operation in this broad area of pastoral ministry and Christian morality.

There are crucial problems—I am thinking especially of problems of conjugal morality—which priests cannot solve without you, without the help of your research and your medical and moral support. We all know the sad problems faced by so many families who have to space their children's births for economic or medical reasons and who suffer because of this. They know the law of the

Church which demands loyalty in conjugal relations and they want to obey it. But they suffer because they cannot harmonize, I will not say love, but one of its expressions, with this law of God.

We have no right to demand that men obey this law without, at the same time, doing everything we can to make obedience possible, without straining all our energies to make the way clear.

There are some sins of intellectual inertia and laziness which will appear graver than sins of weakness at the Last Judgment.

There are several things to be done by research scientists first, then by doctors, to help clear up this saddening dilemma felt by so many good, Christian families—and it is of them only that we are speaking here.

The first, purely scientific, thing is to follow to its conclusion the research begun by some scientists, Ogino and Knaus, for example, in order to determine precisely the female periods of sterility and fertility. Studies on ovulation and the menstrual cycle are of first-rank importance to Catholic homes.

Pius XII, as we all no doubt recall, made the following appeal in his allocution to the *Fronte della Famiglia* ["Family Campaign"] on 27 November 1951 : "We may even hope that medical science will eventually be able to give a sufficiently sure basis for this legitimate method; the most recent information seems to justify this hope."

This appeal should urge us on to continue research in this field. We realize, however, that this determination will not of itself solve the moral problem, which has several aspects, but it will outline the general dimensions of the matter and will help the moral decisions necessary to be clearer, by making the causes behind the choice better known.

On the occasion of this first World Congress, we express the hope that Catholic scientists will urgently bend their backs to this problem which is so vital to the moral health of our homes. The problem should not be insoluble, but it needs everyone's efforts to solve it.

Catholic medical faculties and research laboratories should do all they can, to meet a common need, to extend this research and bring it to certain, definite conclusions. It would be an infinitely valuable favour done to all who are eager to serve our Lord, in marriage and elsewhere, in righteousness and loyalty.

While waiting for science to solve the problem, and even afterwards, doctors still have a great task to do in helping man achieve sexual self-control. This field must not lie fallow. Catholic doctors must continue their investigations and to bring from them, in the light of faith, whatever valuable conclusions they can.

You doctors and research scientists must plan out the roads for your contemporaries, with the sureness of the engineers who planned the St Gothard tunnel and who knew that daylight awaited them at the end of their labours, and you must realize that it will be thanks to you that men will emerge, there too, into the light of God.

It will be noticed that this appeal was for research along two different but converging lines. In the first place, research should be made to ensure man's psychological control of himself, control absolutely necessary for sexual balance.

This is a field where a lot of exploration still remains to be done. Studies and investigations should be intensified so that scientific knowledge already gained, especially in neuropsychology, it seems, can be applied to the field of sexuality. The study of reflexes has shown how far conditioned reflexes may be modified. Could not this be a starting point to begin studying man's basic sexuality, so different from an animal's, and to look for everything possible to help weak wills find the support they need in natural mechanical processes, by means of what is called "psychotechnical training"?

The other, biological, line of research is not concerned with man's control of himself but with control of nature and its laws. This research especially concentrates on fecundity and is polyvalent, inasmuch as it helps promote fertility where sterility exists or is suspected, and can determine with certitude when the sterile periods occur, in order to space births. In themselves, studies like these are good and useful, their moral quality being determined by the intention of the men who make them and those who use their conclusions.

They are very important from a pastoral point of view. Though a small number of exceptional people may be able to practise complete abstinence when some spacing of children is necessary, we cannot impose that as a solution for most Christians. They are often anxious to obey God's law and to avoid sin, but their good intentions need support and encouragement. Anything which can ease the burden of enforced continence by making it last for a shorter time is an inestimable help in keeping souls in the state of grace. Thoughts like these are enough to show how important research into the fertility-sterility cycle of women is as far as concerns Christian charity and even married love.

We all know the different methods, moral and legitimate in principle, which determine the sterile and fertile days of a woman and thereby make a shorter period of continence possible.

The first one was the Ogino-Knaus method, which was later elaborated by Smulders. It has now been completed by the "temperature curve" which, according to scientists, can be used independently of the Ogino-Knaus method and is more accurate. The indisputable value of these methods where a woman's menstrual cycle is normal, is well known, but its application is difficult where the cycle is abnormal or accompanied by anomalies. Though these methods help considerably to make periodic continence easier, there are exceptions, and these are the crux of the scientist's problem.

Scientists have to combine their efforts in order to narrow down the margin of incertitude in exceptional cases as in others. This is a task they were invited to take up by Pius XII, as we have pointed out.

Some work like what we have suggested is being done along these lines at the present time, and it might be interesting to examine it briefly, simply for the sake of information. We cannot make any appraising judgment of this work since a moralist must wait to make his appraisal until scientists have agreed on the conclusions of their work.

In Holland, the Catholic gynecologist Dr J. Holt has been working on the temperature-curve method, as successor to Smulders. In his book, which was recently published in French as *La fertilité cyclique de la femme* (Paris, 1959), he declares that the temperature-curve method is sure, provided it is properly used, and is valid even in exceptional cases. He bases his conclusions on several hundred such cycles, investigated during his long medical career. He says that his discovery lies in having found a key to reading and interpreting the information made available by temperature. He also says that this method, which follows the cycle very closely, makes possible a period of continence shorter than that which must be observed if the other methods are used.

It will be up to scientists to make the final pronouncement on this research. What can be said, however, is that the research of the great German specialist Dr G. K. Döring reached the same conclusions, after he had studied thousands of temperature-curves.

In the periodical *Die Medizinische* (January 1957, p. 5), he writes : "The temperature-curve method is an exceptionally accurate method of determining the fertile and sterile days of the menstrual cycle. My observations of more than five thousand cycles included a single exception only."

To these two declarations we can add the conclusions of

Dr M. Chartier, head of the clinic of the Faculty of Medicine of Paris. Writing in the *Cahiers Laënnec* (December 1954, p. 27), he said :

> We may be impressed by a conclusion which is drawn from an investigation of one thousand and twenty-five cases. The facts were given us by a family counsellor.... On only two occasions he was unable to interpret the temperature-curve, and had to seek medical advice. No pregnancies occurred during the time the method was being used.
>
> We may conclude, then, that this basal temperature-curve method, without being scientifically infallible, nevertheless affords almost absolute security; it could and should, so far as we are concerned, be a good replacement for the Ogino method.

If unanimous agreement is reached on these conclusions, it will be more than ever necessary for doctors, working through trained assistants, to teach the proper use of the method and make it widely known. No matter what it is, every method presupposes a certain, minimal knowledge, and doctors tell us that ignorance on this subject is unbelievable.

One other area of research going on at present is holding many doctors' attention. Because of the margin of uncertainty due to the irregularity of some cycles, research and experiment are now being conducted with a view to "regularizing" irregular cycles or, more exactly, correcting the irregularity by inhibiting ovulation.

In an allocution to the International Congress of Hæmatology on 12 September 1958, Pius XII referred to this research and said:

> The principles applying to sterilization can help in solving a problem many doctors and moralists are pondering today: Is it licit to use pills to prevent ovulation, as a remedy for certain exaggerated reactions of the uterus and other organs, though these pills, while preventing

ovulation, may also make conception impossible? May a married woman still desire to have relations with her husband, despite this temporary sterility?

The reply depends on the person's intention. If a woman takes these pills, not to prevent conception, but simply on medical advice, as a necessary remedy for a disorder of the uterus or other organs, she is bringing on sterility *indirectly*, which is licit according to the principle of double effect.

It would, however, be causing sterility *directly*, which is illicit, if the pills were taken to stop ovulation in order to protect the uterus and other organs from the consequences of a pregnancy which they could not survive.

Some moralists hold that it is allowed to take medication with this end in view, but that is wrong. Equally to be rejected is the opinion of many doctors and moralists that the medication may be used when medical indications are against too short a period between pregnancies or in other cases we shall not go into here. In these instances, the purpose of using the medication is to prevent conception by preventing ovulation; it is, therefore, a question of direct sterilization.

We see, then, that the Church allows a temporary delay in ovulation for a proper medical reason, since that action is governed by the principle of double effect. It is quite otherwise when direct sterilization is involved. Now it remains to determine how far genuine medical reasons can go, and when direct sterilization begins. Moralists are at work discussing the ways to apply these principles.

Added to the research into controlling ovulation is the new research being done into determining the exact moment when ovulation occurs. An intensely interesting article by Dr Doyle, of Boston, has put this question in the forefront of modern research. It does not seem possible, at present, to draw any valid conclusions from the results of this research, which has too early been publicized. Elsewhere, it has been reported that a group of French scientists have discovered a means which is simpler and more precise than Dr Doyle's, but more experimenting will first be done before definite conclusions are drawn. It is enough simply to notice the interest there is in pursuing these studies or other, analogous research projects, since medical science has even more ways to observe ovulation directly.

Added to this medical research, whose final results will be so valuable to priests, we also have the various investigations made into sexual behaviour. Because of its bad method and underlying materialist philosophy, the Kinsey investigation has been justifiably criticized. Everything that men do should not therefore be taken as human and a balance drawn up, as the Kinsey investigators did. Everything that is in nature does not necessarily conform to man's nature, lack of sexual control, for example. Investigations, consequently, have to be carried out on firm bases and with legitimate statistical constants in mind.

Some such investigations are now under way. Catholic science should make itself felt in this field and work towards a better selection, discussion and orientation of material gathered. Some people will recall how effective Villermé's investigation was in the nineteenth century and how it drew public attention to the social question and the wretchedness of the working classes, arousing a reaction in favour of an enlightened economic policy that finally won the day.

A well conceived and thought out investigation, whether conducted by a single group or by several groups along converging lines, which would concentrate on the general climate of human sexuality, could serve to wake people up to reality, as Paul Bureau did in his *L'Indiscipline des moeurs*.

Especially, however, it would be an effective scientific

corrective for the many mistaken ideas which are being handed about and which vague and imprecise knowledge cannot fight. At the present time, every investigator hesitates to publish his findings because his sources of information are too limited. A common effort on the university level or by qualified scientists motivated by the Christian concept of man could do untold good and clear up the morass of error and ignorance.

*   *   *

Quite obviously, there is more than enough work to be done. Everything is to be gained if it is shared in a communal effort, because there is so much of it and because it needs such varied talents. One group of doctors and scientists have appreciated the value of co-operative work among Catholic scholars sharing the same faith and mindful of the same moral questions.

Twenty-eight people, from England, Belgium, Austria, the United States, Holland, France and Italy, answered an appeal made at the Catholic World Congress of Health. They undertook to work under the patronage of the Catholic University of Louvain and study how best to co-operate in man's twofold mastery of himself and nature. The first, private study week-end laid the foundations for various investigations and outlined various projects to be completed. As a result of the exchange of views at the meetings, the group decided to plan periodic, international meetings at Louvain to treat the problems connected with sexology in a Christian context. Like the "Scripture Weeks" which bring together biblical scholars, this communal effort, involving various scientific fields, will be a great boon to encouraging research and supporting the work done in the family life apostolate. It is a step in the right direction.

Chapter XII

THE ROLE OF EDUCATORS

A. Parents

WE now come to those immediately responsible for training in the real meaning of love and self-control: people involved in raising and training children.

First of all, there are parents and, by extension of the parental role, teachers. When they work together they ensure future success: people who train children write a preface to the book of life which is part of life itself. Their influence will be crucial, for better or for worse, according or not as they respond to the obligations laid on them.

Their efforts must be co-operative, because they both work with the same adolescents and young adults. What parents do and what teachers do is all tightly interwoven, and there will be a single result to their common labours.

We begin by examining what can and must be done by parents only and how their role is qualified by certain duties whose fulfilment alone can promise' effective success.

Raising Children

A primary condition of success is the atmosphere in the home. We speak in words, but we say so much more by the atmosphere we create, by our tone of voice, by the way we use certain words, by the thousand unnoticed things of family life. The life that parents have together, as it appears to the watchful eyes of their adolescent children, is a fundamental and indispensable object lesson in life. They will carry the picture of their parents about in their hearts for life; for them, love will mean living harmoniously, with obvious affection, as their father and mother did.

On the other hand, we can expect future catastrophe if a young person's idea of family life is filled with memories of disunity or, far worse, divorce. We need go no further when looking for the reason behind the failure of so many marriages today. A confused and shattered home is a harbour for devastated love, with all its unfortunate consequences ending in children's getting a distorted view of love.

Some recent films are no more or less than illustrated catalogues of the unhappiness which comes from marital disillusion and almost inevitably produces juvenile delinquency. "Teddy Boys" and other delinquents act as they do because, for the most part, they are in disgusted revolt against their youth, when they never saw or received love in their homes.

But if the family atmosphere is full of Christian love, it provides the ideal context for gradual training in love and self-control. Frankness will be easier as will be occasional instruction, following life's natural rhythm which will bring up many opportunities that should be used. We teach so much better when we are not teaching! Everyone knows that students spring to attention when a teacher says that he is going to "digress a bit" and when he knows how to use the art of digression expertly. Daily family life is filled with small events, mealtime chatting, discussion of films which some or all members of the family have seen, argument over a newspaper or magazine article—and all these things allow a slow teaching process which will one day result in a sound and healthy regard for love.

Complete Training

We must remember that this continuous and progressive

training has also to include simultaneously the natural and supernatural education of the child's character and heart. The whole man has to be brought forth, in all his perfection, by using every aspect of his training. An adolescent's character has to be formed and moulded by giving him practical experience in devotedness, courage, a sense of responsibility and forgetting himself and his own interests. At the same time, his religious sense should be developed by encouraging him to frequent the Sacraments and maintain a sensitive conscience. Sex instruction should take place within this well-rounded framework, and should be given clearly and precisely, to ensure harmony and to allow the idea of human love to enter in and take its natural place there.

Parents have the duty of giving this training. Experience has shown, however, that too often they feel ill-equipped for the task.

Unfortunately, the facts show a certain constant failure of parents to give sex education. Not too long ago, an investigation along these lines brought up some significant information. Readers of a magazine were asked to say if, among other things, their parents had told them about the way life begins and the problems of love. Replies, many of them, came from all social levels and were from men and women.

Only seventeen per cent of the husbands who answered, and nineteen per cent of the married women, said that their parents had given them the information they needed. This is not even a fifth! When it came to the question about the problems connected with love, this already low figure plunged even lower. Seven per cent of the men and three per cent of the women answered that their parents had instructed them. Figures like these mean that only the smallest minority of parents are doing their duty.

Parental negligence like this is serious, first of all because they have let slip an opportunity to instruct, but also because children will go elsewhere to find the answers they cannot get at home. "Elsewhere" means the street, school, films, at work or popular literature. This is the exact opposite of training in love's real meaning, it is back-to-front education, and the profanation of love we discussed earlier. Deformation, in this case, will have preceded formation. It is impossible to overestimate the bad consequences of a bad beginning like this.

Speaking about parents' duty to talk about sex with their children, Pius XII said:

> Adolescents should be given adequate instruction in this matter, should be allowed to ask questions without hesitating and ought to get answers to their questions. A forthright, clear and sufficiently explained answer will give them more knowledge and confidence.
> ... Parents can never put aside this responsibility, neither by cowardly disregard for it, nor by a blameworthy silence when the opportunity to speak arises as their children grow and expect legitimate explanation from them (*Documentation Catholique*, 1951, col. 1294).

Why this Silence?

There are several reasons for parents' silence. Here are some of them, not necessarily in any order of importance.

Parents often hide behind the fact that, when they were young, they had no instruction and had to make their own way, and their children should do the same. What a vicious circle that reasoning is!

More often, there is a kind of ill-advised modesty, a tinge of Jansenism or a lack of the right words; the parents cannot express themselves and feel embarrassed. This means that, earlier on, someone else shirked a responsibility: who failed to give these parents adequate preparation, did not help them to express themselves and neglected to give them the positive sexual training which would have made them feel at ease and quite uninhibited in this area?

Frequently, it is simply a case of ordinary irresponsibility, laziness, too many other things to do, the quest for money or pleasure. The parents are too busy to have the time to sit down and think about the problems of educating their children.

In many cases, unfortunately, the hidden reason is even much deeper: because they never had adequate sexual instruction, because they have never really experienced true conjugal love, because, perhaps, their love has even been betrayed within the home, it is distasteful for them to talk about love and sex with their children. Anything connected with sex embarrasses them because it has, somehow, injured them. Here is yet another reason for radical and penetrating sex instruction.

In addition to these faults of parents, there is the other side of the coin. Young people are often slow to talk about these things with their parents.

Conflict between succeeding generations is as old as time and no reason for alarm. Nevertheless, it is important that the transition take place as painlessly as possible and that there be some assurance of basic continuity.

But this conflict can also be caused by a kind of interior isolation which cuts the adolescent off from the people most responsible for his training. A kind of fierce reserve shuts him up in himself at the very moment when he most needs direction and a helping hand.

Too often, a natural dialogue between parents and young people is hindered by the adolescent's natural feelings of independence. It is difficult for him to cross the drawbridge set up between him and his parents by the shyness and awkwardness natural to his age. It is that time of life when he rings the changes on his attitude towards his father, as summarized in this humorous bit:

At the age of ten: "My father knows everything."
At the age of fifteen: "I know as much as my father."
At the age of twenty: "He has really missed the boat."
At the age of thirty: "Still, I wonder what Dad would say."

Parents must proceed carefully, gently and patiently, and look for help from other quarters when it is necessary.

Some people say that the mother should instruct her daughters and the father his sons. Each parent, of course, has some peculiar task that he or she can do better. But if this training is to give the adolescent a balanced picture, both parents should work to complement one another, with mothers talking with their sons and fathers with their daughters.

By taking on their marvellous role as educators in this sphere as well as in others, parents have a unique opportunity of leaving an indelible imprint on the children born of their love. Their children will always be grateful to them for their confidence and for having led them into the kingdom of love with the respect due to a shrine or sanctuary. The natural and supernatural family atmosphere conduces most to the heart's blossoming in the light of the spirit. When they both accept their role as parents, father and mother have already begun the work of harmonizing and have started to give their children the self-control upon which harmony and balance are built.

Parents are not the only ones who must co-operate with and complement one another. Their common activity has to be taken up and continued by teachers.

As he grows, a child spends more time outside his family. School will become more and more important to him. If this education begun at home is to be finally successful, there has to be co-operation between his family and his teachers. Future educational methods will depend more and more on this collaboration.

Co-operative Training

Recent years have seen more and more justifiable emphasis on family-school co-operation, which is necessary from many viewpoints but is absolutely essential in the area we are discussing. If parents are to be the educators we should like to see them ready to be, then frequent and regular meetings of parents will be useful means to introduce them to this task.

Educational meetings open to mothers and fathers will be extraordinarily rewarding, especially if priests, doctors and psychologists, together or on different occasions, can address or speak with them and give them the benefits of their experience.

Being a parent is a marvellous career—and it is very instructive. Too much is left to spur of the moment activity in this sphere, as though young married couples would suddenly discover ready-made solutions overnight. Instinct is a valuable guide, but it needs training and the earliest signs of it should be encouraged and developed.

Meetings will help parents and teachers decide the best way to foster the training and growth of the young people they have in their common charge. If parents themselves do not start to give the necessary instruction, it is up to them to see that someone else does and to satisfy themselves about whomever is continuing or adding to what they have begun. They must not content themselves with vague questions and answers, but should make it a point to find out definitely if the job is being done.

Meetings like these have many things they can discuss: the organization of leisure time and holidays: films, radio, television; instructing young people about the various kinds and degrees of love; their relations with others, friendship, flirtation, parties, dances and balls, social relationships between young men and young women.

As far as they themselves are concerned, parents should

have complete and concise knowledge of the Church's teaching on childbearing as well as on birth control, on artificial insemination and sterilization, on what is legitimate and what is not within the limits of conjugal morality. They have to know all this for their own information and for instructing their grown children. It is a wide world of thought, discussion and education which is opened to zealous teachers.

B. Teachers

If we look at a classical educational programme, we see that young men and women are taught all sorts of things, everything but what is most connected with their vocation as human beings. We prepare them for any and all professions, except the profession of being complete human beings. There is, of course, a movement under way to make our schools more than just centres of instruction, but centres of real education. This movement must be expanded and deepened so that, in particular, education for life will be undertaken positively and systematically.

For one thing, education in chastity is too often negative, and consists of prohibitions. Negative education, of course, is as bad as no education. Negative virtues are not virtues at all. Chastity which consists only in not doing this or that, honesty which consists only in not stealing and charity which is no more than not hurting other people or their feelings, are not chastity, honesty or charity.

Any instruction has to be positive. Besides, it is a question of psychology; instead of being told what they cannot and may not do, young people would rather have help in developing what is best and most generous in themselves. Claudel was right when he said that youth was not made to enjoy itself, but for heroism. A teacher who does not know how to exploit this heroism, does not know the a-b-c of his profession.

Let us say it again: it is not education in love and self-control that is dangerous but lack of this education. Whether we like it or not, this problem is today's biggest and most important problem and is openly discussed everywhere. We have made a lot of progress in biblical studies since the days of St Teresa when biblical study was held to be dangerous to one's faith. The same thing applies here; these problems of life and living have to be examined in the full daylight and true perspective of Christianity. Nothing does more harm than half-truths and a certain narrowness of spirit.

Educators tell us that, where sex instruction is concerned, it is better to speak about it a year too soon than a year too late. St John of the Cross condemned the "sin of taciturnity" of some friars who did not speak during chapter. There is a "sin of silence", just as serious but in a different way, which we must avoid here.

Educators should study this problem of education for life right down to its roots, under the direction of the Church. It is up to them to say what is pertinent or not and to lay out solid lines along which to progress. They have to work out a sort of highway code and draw up the necessary signposts and signals. Such a code, however, will be an invitation to be under way and advance; furthermore, it will need occasional revision as customs and life change. Modern life, if only through television alone, has certainly introduced children and young people to problems which, strictly speaking, fall in the domain of adults. Educators have to take this fact into consideration and not let themselves be outstripped by others who would warp children's ideas and attitudes once for all and drive Christ's grace from their hearts.

Training in our various schools affects the soul, mind,

heart and body of every student. Sexual control is the result of a balance compacted on many levels and in which grace plays a lasting and necessary role.

School Training

It is not enough that a teacher has had one or two, or even several, "good talks" with a student in trouble. Nor is it enough if a retreat master, who is at the school temporarily, has been besieged by the retreatants after a conference in which he discussed these delicate problems. As a matter of fact, the greater the number of students who want to talk to him the stronger the indication that they are not getting all the regular help they need. The instruction should be given gradually and progressively, on all levels. A co-operative, complementary effort will establish a healthy atmosphere and should be deliberately planned by teachers without making the students too aware of it.

There are hundreds of opportunities for putting forth a healthy attitude towards love. Young people will always have many questions about the delicate moral situations they will meet in a course on the Bible, on history or on literature. The questions should not be sidestepped, leaving the students to find answers in a less healthy atmosphere.

A teacher worthy of his profession and well equipped for his job will be able to avail himself of the opportunities for developing sound moral judgments and an appreciation of real love. It needs subtlety, discretion and direct honesty; the slightest hint of facetiousness or frivolousness would be worse than out of place, it would be disastrous. Simply by contrasting love with its counterfeits, a teacher can highlight the wretchedness of sin and its effects. Students will be quick to appreciate this open and forthright approach.

It is much better to bring problems out into the light than to camouflage and conceal them. Truth itself has a function of redemptive purity, provided it is presented as delicately as the matter at hand demands.

Obviously, as both Church and educators agree, this training and instruction cannot be given collectively. The training has to be gradual and finished off in private conversations, according to individual needs. It goes without saying that only teachers properly trained for this indispensable task will be able to do it properly. Schools cannot allow anyone without the proper training, talents and qualities to give this instruction, but should encourage people who give indications of being properly equipped.

* * *

Informal Training

Training such as we have been discussing is not confined to the classroom. There is a lot of work to be accomplished outside.

There is one obstacle to an adolescent's development that has to be got rid of. It is that important turning point in his road to sexual balance when he reaches physical maturity. Frequently, it is accompanied by a more or less long period of masturbation.

We have already seen how widespread the practice is. Adolescents, however, do not really know themselves; they have to be explained to themselves and have the morality of the act put plainly to them. For a sin to be mortal it needs, besides grave matter, full deliberation and complete consent of the will. An adolescent cannot always discern this or, if he can, he cannot make the application to himself. He needs a helping hand to pull himself out of what could become a moral cul-de-sac, if the practice becomes a habit. Teachers will understand that the practice is often generated by a frustration in love or an emotional loneliness the young person has been plunged into, in his own home, perhaps, by the separation of his parents, or by something else. Depth psychology has done valuable exploration and discovery in this field.

Should the difficulty not be resolved, the victim retreats deeper into himself, thereby blocking or hindering his growth towards the gift of self which is the soul of love.

Particular attention should be paid to this problem, especially in boarding schools. If it occurs frequently in an enclosed atmosphere, it should be considered a signal for alarm, and the principals of the school should examine their consciences carefully. One headmistress discovered that the practice was widespread in the school in her charge. She went to a doctor to ask him to see some of the pupils, but he said, "But, Madam, it is not the pupils you should bring to me, but the mistresses."

We shall not go into details of the training which should meet this problem. Let it suffice to urge teachers to make themselves more and more capable by learning and practising the art of helping distressed youngsters along the right road. The final solution, needless to say, will depend upon grace, so that pedagogical methods must be accompanied by the supernatural helps of the Sacraments. But if grace is to be effective, the way must be paved for it by sound pedagogy.

Sex education is something like driving a car. The soul, of course, does not "drive" the body as a driver does a car, but the analogy applies to the psychological attitudes to be developed. The early training must be given in an optimistic atmosphere, putting aside prejudices and preconceived ideas, training the reflexes and overcoming the bewilderment brought on by a complicated situation or the psychological shock resulting from a beginner's awkwardness. Victory here, too, belongs to the man who remains master of himself and his reflexes, with God's grace.

Training in the Use of Leisure

While the teacher works at eliminating obstacles, he should make a positive effort to take full advantage of whatever opportunities there are to influence young adults out·side of school.

Much work can be done by maintaining one's influence over students after school hours. There is a whole complex of social, apostolic, charitable and sporting activities which should be recommended to students. They are first-rate means of forming character and developing control and forgetfulness of self. Nowadays, much of the actual work of training youth is being done by various youth movements where the initial stimulus to generosity and a sense of social and apostolic responsibility is given. After all the appeals made by recent popes, it is something of a scandal that so many schools have yet to introduce these youth movements into their programmes.

Contacts out of school, on holidays, week-ends, camping trips, tours, etc., will give teachers more opportunity to exchange views with their students about their problems; such exchanges will benefit by being adapted to the rhythm of the students' lives. A discussion of a film or a book will bring up spontaneously the chance to pursue the teacher-pupil dialogue, whether it is explicit or not, which is the soul of real education.

We cannot let our young people's leisure time, the use of which will be to their good or hurt, lie fallow and undirected. The study of the educative value of leisure is still in its early stages and would make a fine field of endeavour for teachers with a true love for souls.

Obviously, if teachers are to spend much time with their pupils outside the classroom, a certain amount of adjustment will be needed. Administrators should assign teaching so that no teacher is burdened with too many hours in the classroom and is left with enough time to take care of the other aspects of his role as an educator. Care like this can leave teaching priests and religious free for other work by giving some of their classes to laymen. Administrators who make such arrangements possible will be doing a valuable apostolic action.

Some time should also be left free for contact with families. The sustained and dynamic co-operation which we have seen is important between parents and teachers cannot be restricted to contact between parents and school administrators. All the teachers should carry on the common effort in close genuine unity with parents. The time spent on these contacts is well spent. Some parents will contact teachers on their own initiative, but others will have to be sought out and tactfully brought round to playing their part in the co-operative task or else the whole purpose of education will be frustrated.

Parents and teachers should know one another and work side by side if a child's school training is to be successful and not isolated from his training at home. If parents are not practising Christians, a teacher should try to raise the spiritual tone of the family directly or, indirectly, by putting them in touch with a Christian family movement or with parents of some other pupils.

The obligation put on teachers by their love for souls to mix with their pupils outside the classroom may mean that some semi-enclosed or semi-contemplative communities of teaching nuns will have to modify their rules, to the extent that existing rules hinder their complete apostolic influence. They will have to give up an old fashioned and stilted religious habit for a simple dress more in tune with the customs and tastes of our time.

Everyone knows, surely, that the good of souls can be jeopardized by an exaggerated loyalty to customs and traditions of a different era. A century ago, education could take place "within the enclosure" because social life was more localized and static. People then did not move about as much as we do, and their life was altogether simpler than ours. Life today is not sealed in water-tight compartments but spreads out in all directions. Education has to adapt itself to these changes, to a world that no longer lives in comparative isolation. Today's teachers need a reasonable amount of freedom of movement if they are to have an accurate idea of the world and fulfil their vocation faithfully.

These principles are as valid for women teachers as for men. There is no reason whatever for discriminating between what unordained religious men teachers may do and what teaching women religious may do. Woman's new place in the modern world applies as well to them in everything which promotes the apostolate and education. It is unreasonable to insist that women religious hold on to customs dating from olden days in a world where woman's new position can lead her to high government posts. If apostolic and educational considerations are of no avail in bringing about the desirable changes, then social considerations should prevail : threatening some communities with the charge of being out of date, and, even, with the danger of causing the religious life to lose the respect of the modern world.

If these changes imply greater and more adaptive liberty for teaching Brothers and Sisters, we should not think so much of the possible danger connected with them, as of the greater opportunities for good they allow. Our young people's chastity and life of grace—frequently the two are really only one thing—encourage us to accept the risk underlying every field of the Christian apostolate. A consecrated soul's vow of chastity takes on an apostolic character, which will be its best protection, when it turns itself to the spiritual motherhood or fatherhood of our young people.

Also involved are honesty and justice, first towards the

pupils, but then towards their parents who often make great sacrifices to send their children to religious schools to receive a training they cannot get elsewhere. This special training is not simply training, but a preparation for life and a moral education for love and self-control which is the formation of complete young adults ready for life.

* * *

C. Formation Beyond School

A Painful Situation

A Christian teacher's work does not finish when students leave school. Every year thousands of young men and women leave their various schools and go to work or to universities, where they are brought face to face with the awakening of sexual life and the problems of love. The change is swift and harsh, and too often quite dangerous because their previous education has had little or nothing to say about these difficulties.

What will happen to the young people who have been trained so carefully? Will they swell the ranks of the Christian laity and bring the whole world the full-blooded Christianity it so badly needs? Or will they, as so often happens, go off the rails as soon as they find themselves at liberty in the world as it is? Will they resist the wave of eroticism breaking over their heads?

Experts in touch with young women coming from some of our best schools give us some facts which are saddening but enlightening. According to their figures, only a third of these young women are virgins when they marry and only eight per cent have been able to preserve themselves completely chaste until that time; the others admit that they allow their young men friends every familiarity.

Something else which gives us an insight into the way our young people think is the ease with which they accept flirtation as an unavoidable part of modern life and morals. No one will ever adequately describe the ruin caused by flirtation, a sorry caricature and profanation of love. Love is a deep-rooted committal which obviates pretence or fickleness. Its dignity lies in its integrity, its unity of choice and the lustre of a new and undefiled affection. Love cannot be bought at a discount and the people who try to are the first to suffer. Their hearts and souls remain forever tarnished.

This " ... as if ..." game that more and more young people play is one of the principal causes of love's leaving family life. Here is what one modern expert had to say:

> Young women going out for the first time with young men whom they hardly know, or not at all, feel old fashioned, "out of it", if they do not allow them every familiarity. They are disgusted by their attitude, but do the same thing on the next occasion.
>
> Frequently, after marrying, they allow men other than their husbands the same liberties, since they consider such behaviour natural. They are not capable of the slightest conjugal discipline. Many tragedies develop out of the physical unbalance brought into married life by these practices.

We understand what Pius XII meant when, in his discourse of 8 September 1953, he said:

> Everyone agrees that [young people] have thousands of snares awaiting them in this world which makes them giddy with its hustle and bustle, tires them with its constant restlessness, confuses them with its relativism towards truth and error, good and bad, dazzles them with its bright lights and colours, sullies them with its vulgarity and enslaves them with its lust.

Educators have to take all this into consideration and prepare young people for the dangers threatening them, if they are to preserve love in the hearts of future generations.

The general moral picture of the world, then, is like this and brings on the most wretched consequences: fewer vocations to religion and the priesthood, fewer zealous Catholic Actionists, separation from the Sacraments, faith jeopardized and idealism shattered at life's real beginning.

The Remedy

Everything possible has to be done to correct this situation. Young people crystallize their future moral and religious attitudes between the ages of fifteen and twenty-five, and during those years they need, more than ever, direction and guidance at every stage of this final development. They will look for this guidance and direction to their former teachers who should be ready to do their job, still with discretion but with friendship and firmness. This will be the time to harvest the fruits of previous years' devotion and to bring their mission as teachers to full term. Parents entrusted their children to their care, when they were young, and expect them to influence them as they become adults.

One teacher used to say to his pupils, "I'm not so interested in you as you are now, as in what you will be in ten years"; and a communist, referring to Christian education, once said, "We let you have the children; we'll take over when they're adults."

We cannot ignore young adults; the more vital their problems, the more they need guidance. Young people especially need direction during the two or three years after they leave school, when they run up against the practical side of problems connected with sexual balance and the Christian idea of love. Young men and women begin to go out with one another during this time especially and questions of sexual and marital morality come up. That is above all the time when they need their teachers' help.

These young people have come to grips with the temptations of the world's erotic atmosphere and have, perhaps, met their first defeats. They need a helping hand, a new start before it is too late, to help them to build up everything that will ensure the success of their future homes.

The difficulty is immediately obvious : young men and women leave school before sexual problems are really acute. They may have been given some general advice at the beginning, but contact is too often broken by precisely that time when the influence of their teachers could and should come into play. Teachers see their pupils go off just at the time when life will snap them up and bring them serious problems. They should do all they can to keep up the contact. Loss of contact, of course, may not be entirely their fault, because their pupils will now be feeling the first pangs of a hunger for independence. But at least they can let the pupils know that they will always be available to help.

As we said in our book *The Gospel to Every Creature* (London, 1956), it is important that auxiliaries of the clergy take on the task of encouraging the adult laity to the apostolate. The same is true here: their role with regard to family and marital life is irreplaceable, acting, as they will be, as educators of the young adult laity.

Education has been much too automatic to form real Christians. People have thought that a child's future was assured once his education was finished. It was only a question of leaving adults to their own devices and waiting for results to come in. What actually happened, though, gave the lie to this naïvely calculating attitude. A lot of educational skill has been expended in training children, but far less has been done for young adults. It still needs only the co-operation of all involved to have it develop into what it should be.

A New Outlook

Because of all this, the influence of teachers on their pupils who have left school needs a re-evaluation. They have to do everything they can so that their former pupils take an active part in the various Catholic Action groups within their home parishes. Education is successful when it accomplishes its end—the preparation of Christian apostles, of genuine Christians.

If these former pupils do not join the organizations which so badly need their help to succeed, we shall be correct in fearing that their good intentions, without support and orientation, will gradually fade and that they will join the many Christians who live a half-hearted Christianity; or else they may go so far as joining the downright indifferent.

Teachers have to take care that these young people do enter this organized apostolate and, if such organizations do not exist, they must organize and stimulate them. As they help young adults to live social and apostolic Christianity, they thereby help to prepare good future homes which, in turn, will provide religious and priestly vocations.

From the same viewpoint, our associations for former students also need reorganization. Generally, of course, because former students are so widely scattered, any sort of closely knit and continuous activity is impossible, but the periodic gatherings should be more than occasions for reminiscences and exchanges of new home addresses. They should be used also as opportunities for encouraging apostolic activity and studying the great problems confronting Christians living in the modern world.

Teachers will find occasion to fulfil this role during the social and recreational activities which give them the chance to renew and strengthen contact. Opportunities are many and their love for souls will urge teachers to help their former pupils to a good and fruitful use of their

12

leisure. Teaching communities may also find that they are
encouraged to adapt their rules and customs to modern
needs. Their founders and foundresses worked to provide
education for children who would eventually take their
places in a Christian world. Today, however, these same
founders would be inspired to provide also for our young
adults who are without moral support at the precise moment
of their lives when they turn to be met by a world super-
charged with eroticism and paganism.

Teaching the Teachers

Obviously, all this presupposes that teachers will be
thoroughly equipped for their job. This need is felt everywhere, in mission countries as well as at home.

One priest with wide experience in family matters
recently wrote to me from Africa about the question of
teaching nuns being prepared to give suitable marriage
training: "They must be able to instruct on every level, but
few of them are able to. They have not got the necessary
knowledge or even the vocabulary, and have to leave un-
answered most of the problems which arise."

This evaluation does not apply to Africa only. There is,
at present, a pressing need for a training along clear,
definite lines.

Teachers and professors study to win the degrees and
certificates they need to teach all the many branches of
human knowledge with ability. If such rigorous training is
necessary for the profane sciences, Latin, chemistry, mathe-
matics, etc., why could not faith and love for souls urge
them to hard work and study in the sciences which most
deeply affect man? In the last analysis, have not these quali-
fications been won so that teachers, by means of them,
could be better and more genuine educators of adolescence?
Degrees and certificates are only means to an end. No one
teaches Greek for its own sake, but to train better men for

tomorrow. What we urgently need is a serious and deep training in the study of man.

To get the plan under way and in operation as quickly as possible, could there not be a course or series of lectures on family morality, open to men and women teachers and concluding with a thorough examination to determine whether or not the matter had been thoroughly assimilated and comprehended? A plan like this would make selection and appointment easier. Added to it could be the establishment of teachers' study groups, where they would learn how to discuss these problems with ease and the requisite psychological approach, as well as in simple and direct language, because any tactlessness in talking about such matters can be very harmful. Young women, especially, are sensitive to a careless or ill-advised choice of language.

Plans could also be laid for formative meetings to be addressed by theologians, moralists, doctors, and parents. Everything is to be gained by discussing the subject under all its aspects and by hearing all interested parties put forth their views in their own terms.

Beginnings like these, and others like them, will end the vicious circle that exists because the matter is not talked about since it is so delicate, and it is made delicate because we are not able to talk about it. It is time to stop going round in circles and prepare for the future.

Spiritual Fatherhood and Motherhood

The mission we have just outlined will have high stakes for souls consecrated to God. By their vow of chastity they have renounced the joys of a family, but it gives them an opportunity for a fruitful spiritual fatherhood or motherhood. Their renunciation is the foundation of a marvellous structure, and their total sacrifice guarantees happy and united future homes, and love's sacred character.

René Bazin said that "wherever you find a happy home

you will find a self-sacrificing wife." That is true, but for
this woman to have learned self-sacrifice and devotion, she
will first have had to find a teaching nun who, by her own
sacrifice, has been able to train her in real love. Christian
living begins at one's mother's knee, but that mother has
first to be trained by a consecrated soul who is, through her,
the custodian of the future.

It is a marvellous balance, when religious celibacy and
marriage help one another because, while the renunciation
of men and women religious prepares sound future families,
these families in turn will provide priestly and religious
vocations. Consecrated celibacy—it is the consecration, not
the celibacy as such, which is the victory over selfishness—
is living proof of the parable of the seed which must die if
it is to bring forth fruit.

Adaptations

There is no use pretending that the adaptation we have
been considering will be easy. It will be all the harder because young people are drunk with independence and freedom and will be slow to return to their former teachers on
their own initiative. The flock does not go out by itself to
look for its shepherd; all the more reason for the shepherd to go out after it, and to use all his imagination in
drawing and holding it to himself.

Love for souls, the urgent charity of Christ that St Paul
speaks of, will be greater than any obstacle and will be able
to discover both the means for achieving contact and whatever adaptation is necessary. If the leaven is to help the
mass rise, it must be in it, not outside it. Religious have to
be in the world, though not of it, if they are going to save it.

Active religious congregations have to fulfil to the last
letter their educational and apostolic vocation in this new
area; it means more than bringing the Gospel to mission
areas only. Major superiors of men and women should ask

parents and young married couples what they expect of them and then, along with the proper authorities, study what they have to do in solving the problem facing the destiny of families and the Church.

Most young adults, left on their own at a crucial time, consciously or unconsciously expect help from their former teachers. "I have pity on the multitude," our Lord said when he saw the five thousand in the desert. The same impulse of mercy which impelled Him to perform a miracle will be able, here too, to knock away obstacles and throw up bridges across to those who need help.

By agreeing to expand their hearts, and their rules if necessary, to meet this great spiritual anguish, they will be rendering the greatest service to families and the Church. Putting themselves at the disposal of human love will be helping to restore in men's hearts the image of God, who is Love. Any sacrifice is worth that reward.

Chapter XIII

THE ROLE OF CATHOLIC ORGANIZATIONS

Concentration of Effort

OUR doctrine of life and marvellous, theoretical doctrine on married love cannot simply be treated as rare museum-pieces, kept under glass; everything has to be done to communicate these truths and put them into practice. This is a job for the concerted effort, on every level, of strong and active Christians throughout the world.

If we are going to correct the evils that exist and clear the atmosphere while preparing for human love's return to the state of grace, then we must enlist the forces of all Catholic movements and organizations in the battle. Appeals must be made to leaders of all the different Catholic Action groups, as well as to social, political and intellectual leaders—to everyone who, in America, would be called an "opinion maker".

Every organization has its own role to play in this effort. But that is not all; most of the faithful are not willing simply to be enrolled in any organization, whatever it is. It will not be enough, then, to work with the members of a movement or organization only; they have to be trained to take the message outside the group and share its benefits. More, we should not halt at the boundaries of the Church but go beyond them to enroll men of good will who, without belonging to the Church, are eager to join battle against the moral disorder disrupting families and throwing society off balance.

The Holy Spirit's Inspiration

In addition to the various revivals—apostolic, Marian, liturgical, biblical—taking place in the modern Church, there is also the family revival. It is unquestionably an effect of God's concern for the world, a sign of His saving mercy. We must leave ourselves open to the inspirations of the Holy Spirit and be led by Him. By as close a correspondence as possible with the daily needs of the Church and the Holy Spirit's activity within her, each baptized Christian receives his own full share of grace and his own measure of holiness. People down the various centuries of the Church's history have not all been holy in the same way; our individual ways of holiness are in the Church's holiness, in the graces God gives each day to the Church in our own time.

The family revival would seem to be an inspiration of the Holy Spirit, to whom we must not be disloyal, nor should we sadden Him by indifference, but must give Him our full allegiance.

Family Action in Operation

During recent years, family action, under various names, has gone on within the Church as part of or along with Catholic and social action movements. It is a step forward, and a big one, but just a beginning. On the encouragement of directors of family action groups, several fortunate beginnings have been made.

Pre-marriage conferences or courses have been started almost everywhere; some of them are even correspondence courses. This publicizing of the Christian teaching on marriage has been, often enough, undertaken by teams of workers composed of priests, doctors, teachers and heads of families who work together to highlight the many aspects of the problems which arise. The ways the material is presented are various and are all suitable for spreading the

Christian vision of life. They include forums, study groups and commentaries on films with a love story as their theme.

Retreats for Engaged Couples

From every indication, the days of recollection for engaged couples which have been organized in some places are praiseworthy and a sign of advancement.

Still more can be done, however, because, among other things, these days of recollection just before marriage are rather late to answer problems which may have arisen during the engagement period. Sometimes, the day of recollection comes at the psychologically wrong time, because the couple will have their heads filled with thoughts of preparations, plans, invitations, the ceremony, etc. A retreat must, of course, be made with calm, serene reflection if it is to do any good. More recollection is desirable if the couple are going to profit fully from the short retreat.

Moral Preparation for Military Service

Preparation for love has been broadened recently by the days organized in some places to prepare young men morally for military service. Formerly, these conferences concentrated on the dangers of misconduct, but are more and more being given a positive focus. Their success indicates that they fill a genuine need, and that they should be more widespread so that their benefits may be more generally felt.

This is a marvellous opportunity for chaplains, doctors, even for officers who can bring to bear their own experience of military life and who will be able to use the contacts with their men thus established to gain their confidence.

Family Groups

A direct form of family activity is the family work or study group which gives a better opportunity for similar groups to work among their peers and is a striking example of specialized Catholic Action.

The principal task of pilot-families is to encourage other families to live Christianity completely and to become, in their turn, instructors. The apostolic endeavour to increase and extend the sphere of influence is a counter-agent against the natural inclination to be self-enclosed, or to set up a small, enclosed group. It is moving to attend some of these meetings and see the exchange of views between homes with a common anxiety for determining exactly what is expected of a Christian family, and to feel the air of fraternal simplicity which runs through the discussions.

Some limit, however, must be maintained during these talks. Each family's intimate problems cannot be discussed openly. Christian discretion will show when common discussion must end and when men should talk to other men, and women to women. These groups have also emphasized the need for and value in alternating family retreats with other types of retreats.

Priests as ministers of God will find that part of their role in this apostolate lies in explaining the transcendence and immanence of God's love for men. God is so close to us that He is really ourselves more than we are but, at the same time, His love transcends us so much that it really belongs to another world.

Priests will have to avoid discussing very particular difficulties outside confession or private direction, but their presence will be testimony of the Church's loving care to guide her children along the way of the commandments in daily faithfulness to grace.

Marriage or Family Guidance

Also newly instituted are the many different marriage or family guidance councils in many places. This idea, which is growing today, began in England as a fortunate

*

reaction against the disturbing increase of divorces. The crisis reached its high point in 1947, immediately after World War II, and the British Government was moved to action. A royal commission was established to draw up a plan of action against this social evil. One of its most constructive recommendations urged the establishment of premarital instruction centres and family guidance centres to help families in trouble.

There are other advisory centres, however, which are suspect and conceal harmful propagandizing in favour of family planning through birth control. In the name of eugenic considerations, they teach contraceptive methods with no regard for religious obligations or duties.

Catholics in some countries have realized the danger and have taken it upon themselves to open advisory centres. A priest and a doctor are always on hand to apply the Church's teaching to each case and to work out ways and means of arriving at individual solutions. These centres are powerhouses which organize cycles of conferences, and are an example of what we pointed out in discussing the role of the doctor and the vast area in which his advice can be helpful. We can only hope that there will be more such centres, while we thank and encourage the pioneers who have already taken this first step.

Catholic legal men must realize how great a social evil divorce is and that, for a Christian, it is never a solution which allows remarriage. We run the danger of losing sight of society's common good by allowing ourselves to be thrown out of focus by some few, very sad cases. Divorce is and remains a social plague and hangs over the permanence of homes like the sword of Damocles. Even the fact of its existence brings on a ruinous temptation. Catholic lawyers cannot remain apostolically and socially insensitive when the moral preservation of homes threatened by divorce is at stake.

New Fields of Endeavour

Family action has still a way to go. A broad horizon is open to it, and it has still to take advantage, one by one, of the great means of communication—newspapers, films, radio, television.

Each of these areas needs some moral re-organization. Think of all the cleaning-up and rehabilitation to be done in the field of newspapers, magazines, illustrated weeklies, etc., to mention only one field. Christians are not so much threatened by downright bad literature as by the literature which, without seeming to, teaches a distorted conception of life and love. By words or pictures it stimulates enthusiasm.

Seeing the photo of a film star's fourth or fifth husband, or after reading the detailed history of another actress's divorce, the reader finishes, without realizing it, by admitting that divorce is just part of the way things happen, that love comes and goes, and that children are a nuisance and hindrance to their parents. This kind of reading robs us of our intellectual virginity, which is even more important than our virginity of heart.

The important thing to remember is that it is harder to fight against a wrong idea than an indecent photograph. Everything already said about the ambiguous meaning of the word "love" could be repeated here. Consciences must be sharply refocused to fight against this continuous degrading of love.

All this is the more true when it applies to films and radio and television. They take over homes and fill them with songs and shows that eat away at pure consciences and the sacred character of the only love worthy of that name.

Areas of Influence

A strong reaction must be organized against these on-slaughts, whether they are read, heard or seen.

We need writers who will make love respected and desired without disfiguring and sullying it; poets who will present love in all its true sweetness and loveliness; newspaper writers who will teach a respect for words, without which we cannot have a respect for things; singers who will hymn love on the fresh, pure note of genuine Christian feeling; lawyers have to buttress tottering homes and quench the smoking flax; judges must teach respect for laws even if it means going against popular opinion and running up against the very thing which made St Peter draw back—an ironic smile; factory managers and supervisors have to work to have women respected in their shops, and must fight against the tide of filthy words and ways that threatens to engulf souls that are still pure.

We need members of legislatures who will be on the look-out for anything in laws or institutions that may threaten, or strengthen, the sanctity of our homes; painters should give us pictures of the pure loveliness of the Madonna as the Flemish primitives did; film producers should show us films giving us the glories of genuine love; we need experts to teach our young people to dance as becomes God's children; actors and entertainers should use television or stage plays to talk to men so that love in their hearts is ennobled and dignified.

More advertising people should do what some have already done and use hoardings and billboards to cry out to the world that divorce is a scourge by showing a child torn between his parents, begging them not to leave him; radio and television should broadcast the message of the Gospel, in songs and pictures adapted to modern tastes and styles.

In a word, Christians worthy of the name, no matter in what profession, must testify, as one testifies to the truth of dogma, that love is holy and shrines are not to be profaned.

Lay people, directors of various movements especially, should warn priests, doctors, moralists and lawmakers about threats to home life. They should, if need be, organize meetings to get defence campaigns and counter-influence into operation. They must keep a close watch over people's leisure time, which becomes greater all the time and has a definite influence for good or evil in sex education. Beaches and playing fields have become new mission fields and they need the influence of strong Christian laymen. No sphere of life is outside the sphere of the apostolate.

The Streets

For several years, various groups in different countries have been fighting prostitution. More work of this sort must be undertaken. No single group can hope to accomplish the task, but it can be the pattern and inspiration for similar organizations. Any such movement should be able to call on other organizations for assistance and work hand in hand with them. Each of our organizations should have people experienced in one or another aspect of this whole problem, who would be able to bring their specialized knowledge to the common effort. The American Legion of Decency is an example of what can be accomplished when action is co-operative and orders from directors are carried out.

It is a fact that the Christian conscience has been softened and that it accepts prostitution, especially, as unavoidable. How many active Christians are there who use legal or apostolic weapons against it? Has this pandemic plague— there are between fifty thousand and eighty thousand prostitutes in Paris—been conquered? Are we making a genuine effort to help these poor stray sheep who deserve less blame —the Gospel says so—than the people who take advantage of their wretchedness? Only a handful of people are involved in this work. But Christ is in agony even there, on the streets, and we must not sleep during His agony or pass by without seeing.

Whatever has been suggested as an example of a specialized apostolate can also apply to other types of work, anti-alcoholic groups, for example. Once we realize how responsible the abuse of drink is for sorrow and sexual lapses, then we can only hope that people everywhere will co-operate, in their own way and following their own plan, to fight against alcoholism.

National and International Organizations

At the outset we said that every Christian has a job to do within the Church, through her various organizations and movements. He can also extend his activity beyond the Church's frontiers to work with people who do not belong to the Church. His membership in non-sectarian and official groups, as a private individual but as a Christian, can be an effective influence in protecting and fostering the moral value at stake.

The first principles of family or marital morality can be brought into play constantly within these organizations. It can happen more than once that an administrative decision, though apparently inoffensive perhaps, will advance or hinder our cause. Christians should make themselves felt wherever souls are at stake or where Christ's life in them can be destroyed or developed. This applies whether the organization is national or international. Recent pontiffs have been right to insist that Christians must take part in key organizations influencing and, to some extent, controlling the destiny of the nations of the world, such as Unesco, the World Health Organization, the International Union of Family Organizations, and many others.

These groups hold in their hands the present development of nations and their future destinies. Christians working with others in these movements—and the value of such collaboration can often be pleasantly surprising, because of the many and diverse problems arising—could prevent an anti-family proposal's taking on the force of law for whole continents. In one case, they have already reached a dangerous turning point within Unesco and prevented a further and irretrievable victory for neo-Malthusianism.

We shall not recount what has already been done, courageously but unsteadily. Let it suffice to point out what still remains to be accomplished—a whole world to create, in every sense of the word.

CONCLUSION

GOD said, "You shall love...."

God's whole law is in the words, "You shall love...." This love goes in two directions, towards God and towards our neighbour, but it is one love, not two. *Duo praecepta, sed una caritas,* said a Father of the Church; there are two commandments, but a single love motivates them.

Our purpose in this book has been to preserve and revive the holiness of this love in the face of human weakness. The Devil has done everything he can to profane love and prevent Christians from talking about it and carrying to the world, like a torch in the night, the pure doctrine of genuine love sprung from God's heart. What a tragic situation we have seen, in which educators and teachers, parents and many other Christians whose mission it is to speak out have been silent.

Our Lord's words, "The truth shall make you free," are more true and necessary here than elsewhere. If we rediscover the real meaning of love, we shall find the true liberty of the children of God.

You shall love.... The Gospel is nothing more than a development of this theme.

Love is the beginning of Christian life because, at baptism, the Holy Spirit pours into our souls a new love, theological charity. It will also end our lives, because the Last Judgment will be based on one question: What have you done with the love that should have set your heart aflame? Love runs through the course of life like a thread. Our Lord meant the fire of love when He said, "I have come to cast fire upon the earth, and what will I but that it be kindled?"

We must guard the flame God has given us after lighting it, like a living torch, at His own heart. We must hand it on to others; each home is a relay station which has to carry this warmth and light a little bit further.

People who renounce human love for a higher love of God and men do it only to teach their brothers how to protect the flickering flame from the many gusts threatening to extinguish it.

You shall love. . . .

The cardinal virtues are nothing if charity is not their soul. Justice without love is a denial of justice because, as Joubert said, man can be just only to him whom he loves. Prudence without love is spiritual niggardliness because it does not deserve its name unless it will take risks to love even more. Without love, fortitude is brutality, because true strength is simply love that desires to promote good and ensure its final victory. Temperance without love is mediocrity and empty show, because self-control must be in love's service. This is the real meaning of chastity in God's eyes.

You shall love. . . .

It is a sentence as simple as God Himself, and brings a life to unity because what God wants us to do is love all our brothers, as well as Himself, with one, selfsame love.

Love spreads out in concentric circles, ever broader, to the ends of the earth. Our next-door neighbour is gradually replaced by our neighbour in a distant country. But we must love them all with the same love.

Love's operation will vary, just as God's love is varied. It will be differently expressed in different situations and according to the degree of intimacy they engender. Love's manifestation extends from a married couple's union to the smile and handshake that greet a stranger. It is, however, a matter of variations on a single theme. Love's demonstrations are a single dynamism, beginning in God and returning to Him by means of the many ways of being faithful to His law.

You shall love. . . .

The sentence shines like the star that led the Magi from the East; it is the apostolic standard on which God wants us all to discern the true face of His Church and disciples.

"See how they love one another," was the first argument that convinced the crowds of Jerusalem when they saw the early disciples, and it converted thousands of them.

"Look at the love I am teaching you," the Church has said to successive generations, "and realize the price it costs me." Did she not lose England, during Henry VIII's time, rather than sacrifice the indissolubility of love that our Lord had entrusted to her maternal heart; is she not ready to see herself deserted by the many who find her words too hard to bear and turn their backs on her?

But she is always ready and hoping to open her arms wide to her prodigal children who have eaten of worldly food and are hungry and nostalgic for their father's house. Think of the young Scandinavians who, after having run the gamut of the world's pleasure, said to a visiting priest, "Our only choice left is between the Catholic Church and suicide."

You shall love. . . .

It is an appeal the Church makes to modern men to bring them to re-discovering what they are missing more every day: joy in their hearts.

Open or secret sexual disorder is mainly responsible for men's unhappiness. Moral failure weakens, enervates and depresses. Uncontrolled searching for pleasure smacks of the unreal, the meaningless. Only self-control and obedience to God's commandments can lead men into the kingdom of true joy, always new and unexplored, like God

Himself. We have to choose. Nature takes it upon herself to point out to us our true end, as Bergson said:

> Philosophers who have speculated on the meaning of life and on the destiny of man have failed to take sufficient notice of an indication which nature itself has given us. Nature warns us by a clear sign when our destination is attained. That sign is joy. I mean joy, not pleasure. . . . Wherever there is joy there is creation; the richer the creation, the deeper the joy. The mother beholding her child is joyous, because she is conscious of having created it, physically and morally. . . . He who is sure, absolutely sure, of having produced a work which will endure and live cares no more for praise and feels above glory, because he is a creator, because he knows it, because the joy he feels is a divine joy.[1]

* * *

Thus it may happen that we shall see in a new light the words of our Lord, "My yoke is sweet, my burden light," that are often made a complaint against the intransigence of the Church.

No matter how tragic and incomprehensible a situation may seem, this sentence remains valid. It may be necessary, however, to see it in the light of faith. Heavy lowering clouds can hide the sun so that we almost imagine it no longer exists, but the sunlight of faith is constant, faithful and sure.

This can be a peaceful and joyful realization for people in difficulty, because our Lord's words remain true despite appearances to the contrary and are true no matter how times or situations change. Nothing can happen to put the lie to these words which control and dominate events. If need be, they are powerful enough to be miraculous, if we

[1] Jacques Chevalier, *Henri Bergson*, trans. Lilian A. Clare, London, 1928, p. 260.

only submit ourselves to them, as our Lady did when she expressed her complete obedience to God in her *Fiat*. The truth of the words entered deep within her and formed her; the joy she expressed in her *Magnificat* is an expression of her fidelity.

Every Christian who obeys God's law holds the key to joy and serenity to the extent that he obeys the commands of the law as a child. Christianity, as such, is the wellspring of happiness for individuals, families and society. When we live the law of the Gospels to the letter, we feel the peace and joy which our Lord said "the world cannot take away" because the world does not know it.

This applies especially to God's law of marriage: control and forgetfulness of self, a law of faithfulness and permanence which seems a bitter trial to human selfishness and fickleness. Humanity's family happiness cannot be bought at any other price, despite contrary appearances and some situations which are, humanly speaking, beyond hope and temporarily insoluble. Here, more than elsewhere, obedience must spring from deep theological faith.

One Christian of clear and courageous faith was looking for a better understanding of his duties in marriage and wrote the following lines to me. They are a remarkable, living witness to our Lord's promise.

The only thing I want to know is what God's will is in this matter, because no matter how apparently difficult obedience to His will seems to someone judging from the outside, it is the only sure and easy way.

The man who obeys gets the necessary graces and they give life to his soul. Only the weight of sin is a heavy burden and weighs down body and soul as it grows. The yoke of our Lord remains sweet and light when it is accepted completely; no man can take away the soul's supernatural joy coming from God.

Every kind of martyrdom, even its least spectacular

form in family trouble, can be easily borne. If we find it hard to understand how His 'yoke is sweet' and His 'burden light', isn't it because we forget that love makes even the most difficult burden sweet and light?

Our Lord is Incarnate Love and comes into our souls, giving us joy that nothing created, no matter what it is, can take away, neither deceit, betrayal, disappointment nor frustration. We have a secret place inside us where joy reigns unchanging. I have felt it all through my life so strongly that I can say that I have never known suffering because I have never suffered.

The only real suffering is the martyrdom of a soul without faith, hope or charity.

Not everyone can reach this highly developed, logical theological faith. Every Christian must work towards it, however, convinced that it is the price of peace of heart and joy. A Christian realizes that he is working towards his final goal and that he will achieve peace, if he obeys God's will for him, this will which is not capricious but is the very expression of God's love for him. This joy outshines all pleasure, as the sun does artificial light. Christians owe the world a witness to this joy, born of the Holy Spirit and the fruit of grace-filled love.

* * *

We began this book by saying that it was written for everyone who has a direct responsibility in training others for love. Now that we have come to its close, we turn to married couples to ask them to be courageous and unsparing in handing on the torch of love to future generations. We put this invitation in the form of a few lines we addressed to some engaged people just before marriage.

I was in an aeroplane, returning to fly over a large city with all its lights ablaze in the night. It looked like a tremendous Milky Way fallen to earth. Each house sent out its own beam of light and the whole thing looked like a torchlight procession frozen into immobility.

I was thinking about some young friends of mine who were going to be married shortly and who, in their turn, would be a light shining in the darkness, a candle to be held on high rather than hidden beneath a bushel. After leaving the aeroplane, I wrote the following to them, which will end this book and repeat to every family, known or unknown, the eternal message of happiness and love, of happiness in love, which lies within the heart of Christianity:

Look down on a city from an aeroplane.
You cannot really measure men and things
    as they are from up there.
Ask yourself what each of those houses means,
    and the secrets of all those blocks of flats.

What is a house?
The shelter for a home.
The shelter may be poor or luxurious,
but its treasure is always the same: a home.

But what is a home?
The meeting of two loves.
A young man and woman who met one day.
Their meeting was arranged, after many mysterious
    chance encounters,
by what we call Providence.
The man and the woman said something very simple
    to one another : "I love You."
Because there are no other words, and it means the same
    in every language.
Rich and poor say it in the same way,
because here, at least, everyone is really equal.

But why did *these* two meet?
Who can say?
The man will give reasons,
and because he wants to be reasonable, he will think of
        reasons for loving her
and will repeat these reasons to himself and his friends
        —if they really want to know them.
But his friends will not put too much stock in his
        reasons—how wise they are!

The woman will not explain;
She loves because she loves. Full stop. Nothing more.
Her love will be steadier because it is not built on a
        foundation of reason and discussion

A home is born from these two loves.
It is like a hearth where two fires burn, far from the
        threats of stifling wind.
One day, these two flames will bring forth another
        flame, then still another.
A home is like the cave at Lourdes,
with thousands of little candles
surrounding a big one that protects them.

The flame is love,
and each candle is a reserve of love.
The flame exists in God's image.
Because God is Love.
And everything that is really real
that happens in each of these houses shining in the
        night
touches the life of this flame
Man was not made except for that.
So was woman.
And children.
And their children's children.

They must guard the Love of God in precious coffers.
There is no better way to protect it than by sharing it.

Who would save love—like the man who would save his
        life—must lose it.
Lose it in other souls,
who will have life from this gift
for time and eternity.
Because Love does not die,
since God is immortal and
it is God who loves in men's hearts.